Bi

MW01105423

Biography of a
Business Legend
and
Philanthropist

By
Steven Eckard

Table of Contents

Introduction

Many people have said many things about life, and there are numerous definitions of life in the dictionary. The simplest of these definitions is; "the period during which a person is alive". In the simplest terms, life is the period between a person's birth and their death. And while every person goes through the same life stages of birth, childhood, adulthood, and death, some people accomplish more during their lifetime than others. Their impact on the world lasts long after their physical existence on earth ends. So in a way, they live eternally. And their stories, well that is the stuff legends are made of.

Bill Gates is, without question, one of the world's most outstanding personalities. He has created a legacy for himself that is granted to outlive him. This biography covers the life of a man who has dominated the computer software industry with the world's biggest software company and amassed a huge personal fortune. What shaped him into the philanthropist he is now? How did his early childhood prepare him for the later stages of his successful life? And in a detailed study of the business maneuverings of Bill Gates, another question always arises; to what extent would you go to win? With this text, I hope that you will understand not just the makings of legends, but also the small things that define the lives of legends.

Family Background and Childhood

A few minutes after 9:00 p.m. on the evening of 28th October 1955, William H. Gates Sr., a prominent Seattle lawyer, and his wife Mary Maxwell Gates welcomed their second-born child, a boy, into the world. They named him William Henry Gates III. His family would christen him Trey, but the world would know him as Bill Gates, the man who would at one time in the future command the world's greatest fortune and whose name would be synonymous with Microsoft, the world's largest software company.

Bill Gates is known for being a self-made multi-billionaire, having built a large fortune from scratch over the course of several decades. His self-made tag becomes even more impressive when you discover that he had been bequeathed with a million-dollar trust fund which he chose not to use, choosing instead to bootstrap his start-up company. Greatness was in Bill Gates' blood from the very first.

And while he could shun the trust fund, his pedigree was inescapable. The family on his mother's side, the Maxwell's, could trace its roots to Iowa where its patriarch J.W. Maxwell, Bill Gates' great-grandfather, had been born in a farm. At the age of 19, J.W. Maxwell moved to the town of Lincoln in Nebraska and joined the banking industry, starting out as a teller and rising up the ranks. In the year 1882, he moved to South Bend, Washington on a colleague's suggestion. There he started the National City bank and built it into one of the most prominent banks in the region before pursuing a political career; first as town mayor and later as a representative in the Washington legislature.

His son James Willard Maxwell went to the University of Washington in the 1920s to pursue a business course. There he met his future wife, and after graduating in 1925, he joined his father at the bank, first as a messenger and later, after having risen through the ranks, as its leader in his father's place. The family was prominent in the Seattle high society, with Maxwell's wife participating actively in community organizations. Mary Maxwell was born in 1929, was brought up in the high society of Seattle and grew up as an active child and a good student all the way to the University of Washington.

The family on his William H. Gates' side of the family was less high-flying. His grandfather was a carpenter who operated a furniture store in Bremerton. Bill Gates' father had enlisted in the army as soon as he graduated from high school in 1943 to fight in World War II. After his discharge in 1946, William H. Gates Sr. joined the University of Washington to pursue a law degree.

Mary Maxwell and William H. Gates Sr. were introduced by a student leader named Brock Adams and started going out. In 1950, William Gates graduated and started practicing as an assistant in a Bremerton law firm. Two years later, Mary graduated and followed him to Bremerton where they were married a few months later. Their first child, daughter Kristi, was born shortly after their marriage in 1954.

With such great wealth, the family on Bill's mother's side was naturally well connected. Mary Maxwell herself would go on to serve on the board of prominent corporations like Pacific Northwest Bell and the First Interstate Bank.

Bill enjoyed the idyllic childhood of an only boy born into an upper-middle-class family. To add to Kristi, a younger sister named Libby was born 9 years after Bill's birth.

While he is naturally very intelligent with the IQ of a genius, Gates developed many of the traits from his childhood the world would later come to identify. For example, he had already read the World Book Encyclopedia from cover to cover by the age of eight. He also started the habit of rocking himself on the cradle, a habit that persisted into his adulthood and became something of an inside tradition for Microsoft programmers emulating their role model.

The most influential habit that Bill formed in his childhood, however, was competition. He had the compulsive craving to be better than everyone else, be it in games, school assignments, writing papers, or practicing on a musical instrument. It was not enough to be the best though; Bill ensured that he did everything to the max, whether it was a 30-page report on the human body when the teacher had asked for 4-5 pages or playing, and winning Demolition Derby in bumper cars against adults.

And it was an easy trait to develop because Bill's parents encouraged their children to be competitive. There were always rewards for the winners and a penalty for losing, often involving extra chores. An Olympics tournament of games was often organized for the family where they competed at racing, tennis, and a custom-made game of "Capture the Flag" that tested the participants' mental as well as physical abilities. So, whether Bill developed his fierce competitiveness from the environment he grew up in or it was inborn, may not be easily verifiable. It was probably a combination of the two; a naturally competitive boy whose skills were sharpened to an art form by his parents.

Bill had always loved reading from a young age. While other nine-year old boys consider homework and study an assignment, Trey would read ahead and read extra books just because he could. By 8, he had already read the encyclopedia from cover to cover. A sharp photographic memory allowed him to retain most of what he read.

William and Mary Gates grew concerned that Bill's out-of-the-charts intelligence would impair his social skills. Being a boy who could stay in his own company reading in his room for hours on end, his parents were quite right to be worried about his social life. To give him the opportunity to interact with boys his own age, they signed Bill up for the Boy Scouts. While he was fairly active as a member, it would be an exaggeration to say that Bill developed top-notch social skills. What he did learn to do was to persevere amid excruciating situations, an

Aurelian kind of stoicism.

During one summer hike, Trey had arrived at camp with a brand new pair of hiking shoes that turned out to be one size too small and hurt his feet when he put them on. Despite the pain that would turn to blisters and openly bleeding wounds, he stoically persevered through the 30-mile hike. His fellow boy scouts eased his burden by carrying his backpack for him. It was all they could do after Trey stubbornly refused to abort and allow someone to take him back to camp for first aid and maybe a more appropriately sized pair of shoes. By the time he arrived at the next checkpoint, he needed urgent medical attention and his mother was called to cart him away.

Bill's parents encouraged their children to ask them anything about their work at the dinner table. Discussion was encouraged, with most issues being up for negotiation if one could find the right way to convince Mary Gates, the parent who was always around while her husband built his law career with long hours at the office, that it was the right thing to do. Bill and his father had a rather distant relationship until later, when they learned to depend on each other for the really important things. Years later, when Bill was starting Microsoft, his father would give him legal advice and help him draft legal documents when he didn't want to splurge on a lawyer.

All these subtle acts and traditions obviously implanted on Trey's mind the notion that winning was the most important thing and allowed him to develop an open view of authority devoid of any mysticism.

The Gates family worshiped at the University of Washington Congregational Church. Trey attended a confirmation class taught by Reverend Turner, a pastor from Lawrence. In 1966, just like he did every year, Reverend Turner challenged his confirmation class and the congregation to memorize the Sermon on the Mount, one of the hardest passages of the bible to commit to memory. Those who could accomplish the mean feat would be rewarded with a free dinner at a restaurant located 600 feet in the air at the Space Needle which had been built in 1962 as part of the World Fair held in Seattle.

Bill Gates was just 11 years at this point, but he had a thing going for him that no one else at the UoW Congregational Church had; an almost photographic memory and an unquenchable drive to win. When the Reverend came to the

Gates' home to listen to Trey try to win the free dinner like so many others, he was surprised by the eloquence with which he recited the passage. The reverend had never encountered anyone who could make it through the whole passage without faltering. Bill Gates did not stop to collect his mind and neither did he trip. And so at the tender age of 11 years, Trey experienced once again, the euphoric feeling of besting people older than himself.

That same year, his parents decided to enroll him to Lakeside school. His intellectual superiority was unchallenged in the public school where he had been schooling with his sister Kristi. His parents reasoned that a private prep school would challenge this genius boy's dominance in math and science better.

Lakeside school turned out to be a turning point in Bill's life because not only did he develop an interest in computer software and meet Paul Allen, Microsoft co-founder there, he also met many of the best programmers that would help propel Microsoft to the heights.

Chapter 1: Lakeside School

Lakeside school admitted the brightest and the most outstanding boys in the Seattle area, and at $5,000 in tuition fees, most of these boys were from the more wealthy and powerful families. Bill joined Lakeside just as it was experiencing changes from its hitherto classic prep school uniform of proper coats, ties, and wingtip shoes.

The environment at Lakeside was exactly what a boy like Bill needed. It was highly competitive, non-conformist, and the administration encouraged students to form and nurture interests out of the mainstream curriculum. When he arrived at Lakeside, Bill's only claim to fame was his small body and big feet. Soon, the boys at Lakeside would all know his name.

In 1968, America was at the threshold of its space exploration age. Computer technology had made it possible for the space agency to consider making manned flights to the moon. It was becoming more and more important for students to receive training in the use of computers, and Lakeside school was prepared to lead the way.

Unable to buy a computer, the school decided to

approach the problem creatively. By buying a teletype machine and installing it in school, students could operate a General Electric (Program Data Processor) PDP-10 minicomputer located in Seattle. The school was billed for computer time. An initial kitty of $3,000 had been raised by the Lakeside Mothers Club, intending the amount to last for at least year.

Lakeside school was divided into the lower and upper schools. Seven and eight graders were in the lower school, with nine to twelve graders being the upper, more privileged members of the Lakeside school student fraternity. They could smoke, they could use the front doors, and even the teletype machine was housed in the upper school. As such, the upper schoolers received special privileges to use the machine.

Bill first saw the computer room during a math class. Under his teacher's supervision, he entered a few commands on the machine, and, a few moments later, received a response. He was hooked from the very first day. Henceforth, any free time he had, Bill competed for computer time with a bunch of equally intrigued upper schoolers, among them a boy two years older than Gates by the name of Paul Allen.

The $3,000 kitty was soon spent, forcing the school to ask the student's parents to pay for their sons' computer bills.

Bill Gates, however, had finally found the machine that would become his life. With characteristic devotion, he pored over any materials that taught him how to use computers, thriving in the computer room environment that had a pitiably inept teaching fraternity. He was quick to master the Beginner's All-purpose Symbolic Instruction Code (BASIC) computer language developed a decade previously by Dartmouth College professors.

At 13, Gates wrote his first program that enabled him to play a game of tic-tac-toe on the computer, followed soon thereafter with a moon landing game. Becoming even better at the BASIC language coding, Gates wrote a program that enabled him to play Monopoly against the computer, even teaching himself to play better by having the computer play thousands of rounds of Monopoly to come up with winning tactics.

In the classroom, the exceptionally gifted Bill was soon good enough at math that he was taking advanced University of Washington math courses. In fact, he was so good that he could be excused from the classroom to spend time at the computer room and still perform better than his colleagues.

The computer room became the nucleus from which would emerge a friendship and partnership rivaled by few others. It was the potent combination of soft-spoken and sociable Paul Allen and the fiercely competitive and driven Gates. After spending numerous hours at the computer room and challenging each other to try highly advanced operations on the PDP-10, the two became fast friends. Their adventures in the business of computer operations would start in school and eventually pour out into the outside world.

The computer room gang had mastered the PDP-10. They were even more skilled at programming than their teachers at Lakeside. A new player had come into the scene, offering the programmers of Lakeside an even larger pool of computer time than the General Electric computer could allow. Computer Center Corporation, which the Lakeside gang would christen C-Cubed, owned a number of leased PDP-10 computers on which it sold time on to interested parties more cheaply.

C-Cubed computers had a somewhat superior set of software, one which allowed the user to run a task in the background. Gates and co. used this feature with reckless abandon, racking up huge bills that they tried to conceal by hacking into the security system and altering their bills. They were caught, reprimanded, and suspended from C-Cubed for six weeks.

The PDP-10 operated on very defective software. After writing his first program on one of the C-Cubed PDP-10, Gates, over a period of several days, caused it to crash multiple times. He would later discover that the reason for the computer's repeated crashing was his typing "Old program name is Bill" to call up his software package while he was supposed to type simply "Bill."

At the same time when C-Cubed was experiencing numerous breakdowns that were threatening their business, Gates and Allen were both discovering each other's passion for computers. They both felt strongly that computers would be the future, which is probably the reason why they clicked so well in the first place. Their continued mastery of BASIC programming would ultimately bring out in Bill the one quality that he needed to become the man the whole world came to know.

Bill Gates' own programming from childhood had been that of pushing boundaries, being better, excelling. Paul Allen and Bill Gates invited a friend each; Richard Weiland and Kent Evans respectively, and started a ragtag entity they called the Lakeside Programmers Group. The sole aim of the group was to sell their skills in computer language to the "real world" and make some money while at it.

Steve Russell, part of the C-Cubed team of programmers, came up with a solution for their computers' unreliability. They would need a team of friendly users to help them discover bugs in their systems and avoid the numerous crashes that dissuaded paying customers from using their machines.

It was the perfect set-up. C-Cubed benefited from the diligent exploits of the Lakeside four and discovered (and solved) numerous bugs on their computers. The Lakeside Programmers Group, on the other hand, could use all the computer time they wanted for free. And what's more, their job was to push the PCP-10 to the extreme to discover what caused it to crash.

A new craze was born. A day and night lifestyle of programming Bill Gates called "hardcore." Years later, the hardcore lifestyle of night and day programming would be popularized at Microsoft.

The four boys were eager to learn everything they could about computers, but it was Bill Gates and Paul Allen who showed the greatest dedication. The two learned anything and everything that they could about not just the computers, but also, and more importantly, the software that made the gadgets come to life. Software, they recognized, was the "soul" of computers.

They pestered Russell, the C-Cubed programmer who often stayed in the office late at night and monitored them at work, with questions. He eagerly answered their questions and often allowed them to read software manuals they were not supposed to read. Russell would later recall that Bill and Paul were "more interested in breaking the system than Wieland and Evans." Their names featured more than anyone else on the "Problem Report Book," a journal they were required to fill detailing the cause of bugs as they occurred during their computer use.

Gates and co. had made a deal that allowed them to enjoy a pastime that would have otherwise cost them a fortune. C-Cubed, however, was struggling to stay afloat. In 1970, the company folded. Leaving Allen and Weiland in the dark, he and Evans bought the C-Cubed computer tapes at a bargain price. Allen was not amused by their antics. He confiscated the tapes, but Gates eventually got them back and sold them and made a nice profit. This is the earliest indication of Bill Gates the shrewd businessman who would later make some very astute deals as the head of Microsoft.

The next business deal the Lakeside Programmers Group made was with Information Sciences Limited, a company that operated on a business model similar to C-Cubed out of Portland, Oregon. Allen and Weiland usurped this new project for themselves, asserting that there was not enough work for the whole group to come on board. Of course, it was also sweet payback for the younger students' profiteering antics during the C-Cubed closure.

However, the two soon realized that they were in way over their heads. They were easily distracted, neglecting their work to explore the computers' intriguing software. They asked Gates and Kent Evans to come back. Bill would only come back under one condition- he would be in charge of the project henceforth. It was the first program he worked on using Common Business Oriented Language (COBOL) and the group was paid yet again in computer time.

The year after the Information Sciences Limited deal, in 1971, Paul Allen finished his high school education but kept in touch with his Lakeside school buddy Bill. They had already started another company, this time as a duo, called Traf-O-Data. The boys had created a program to analyze traffic data and sell it to municipal authorities for traffic planning. By using a computer rather than the medieval traffic boxes used before, Traf-O-Data churned out data faster than their competitors.

Traf-O-Data was the first all-out business Bill and Allen were involved in. The company hired Lakeside students to help with data transcription and other menial tasks. Bill and Paul went as far as attempting to build their own computer from scratch. They enlisted the services of a Boeing engineer and called it the Traf-O-Data machine, but they could not make it run reliably. Nevertheless, Traf-O-Data brought in about $20,000 in the few years it was operational.

While Bill was showing an increased capability in programming, it was the business of computer programming that seemed to interest him most. Trey was never short of business ideas, and he always followed through with a venture. With the Lakeside Programmers group now reduced to a twosome after Paul and Wieland graduated, Bill and Kent consolidated into Logic Simulation Company. They immediately started a recruitment drive around school that culminated in the Logic Simulation Company being contracted by the Lakeside school administration to computerize the class schedules.

Unfortunately, Kent Evans was not to live long enough to start work on that project. He died in a freak accident while out on a mountain-climbing trip on Memorial Day Weekend. Bill enlisted the services of his friend Paul to continue the project. The two would later dedicate an auditorium in Allen Gates Hall, a building they co-sponsored in Lakeside school, to Kent Evans.

Bill the astute businessman Gates continued to manifest the following summer when he served as a page in the US House of Representatives. Having bet on the wrong candidate for vice president and bought 5,000 McGovern-Eagleton buttons, Bill stood to lose money when George McGovern decided to go with the US

France ambassador Sargent Shriver for vice president. Instead, Bill repackaged the buttons as keepsakes, sold them at $25, and made a handsome profit.

Bill was now actively marketing his services as a programmer. With the few successful gigs he had under his belt at this point, he started a marketing campaign, sending letters to local schools with the offer to digitize their class schedules. The only job he got was from the University of Washington Experimental College, but it fell through when the student magazine discovered that Bill was Kristi's brother. Not only was she a student at the university, she was also an official in the student association. The revelations scuttled the whole deal, costing Bill a lot of money.

So far, despite numerous tries and varying degrees of success, Bill had not yet made good money from his programming work. He was desperately eager to earn some 'real' money. Fortune was about to smile down at him.

At the same time, Bill was hunting for money making avenues to put his programming skills to work, Paul was becoming increasingly fed-up with life at Washington State. 160 miles away, the Bonneville Power project was in trouble.

TRW, the company contracted to write software for the computers that would regulate electricity generation and supply, was using the PDP-10 computer to write software. They faced the same problem C-Cubed had faced a year prior, taming the frequent crashes caused by bugs in the system. By chance, TRW employees found the C-Cubed Problem Report Book, filled to capacity with bug reports, a majority of which has been written by two programmers named Paul Allen and Bill Gates.

After interviewing at TRW headquarters in Vancouver, the two boys were hired. Their weekly salary would be $165. Lakeside school was gracious enough to excuse Bill for the second term of his final year while Allen left his classes at Washington State altogether. For three months, the two hunted for bugs in the TRW computers, fixing them to make the computers crash-resistant as stipulated in TRW's contract.

It was a very beneficial experience for young Gates, building him as a programmer in ways that other jobs had not. His job in this gig was to hunt and fix bugs- to improve the software and make it more reliable. It was training that would become very useful later on. Gates also picked up a habit that would make him notorious at Microsoft later on.

Among the many people Paul and he worked with at TRW was a programmer called John Norton. He was one of the best at TRW and he and Bill instantly hit it off. Bill learned a lot from Norton including the art of the critique. You see, Norton had the habit of commenting on code written by his colleagues, emailing them at all times of the day and night with sarcastic and critical opinions. Bill Gates copied that habit and would end up sending numerous such memos to Microsoft employees later on.

But first, Bill had to race back to Lakeside for his final exams. Jumping back into schoolwork in time for his final exams proved to be relatively easy for the gifted Bill. Not only did he catch up fairly easily, but he also aced all his exams. He had already been accepted to Harvard earlier that fall. All he needed to do was to graduate.

Before proceeding to Harvard, Bill ducked back to Vancouver. The TRW project was still ongoing. The summer brought with it the first dreams of forming a software company, not just as a hobby, but to write serious software for the expanding computer market.

Chapter 2: Harvard

Finding your interest is null if you do not pursue it. Success comes from pursuing one's thing with dogged determination and the beginnings of this pursuit is a very important stage in your life. Pursuing your life's interests is an exciting and scary prospect, and that is why many people procrastinate.

While James Wallace and Jim Erickson state that Bill Gates' "arrived at Cambridge in the fall of 1973 with no sense of what he wanted to do with his life..." (1992) it is clear that his time at Harvard was simply extended procrastination. He knew exactly what he wanted to do. He felt the push to follow his passion for programming and marry it with his business acumen and start a software company. He had discussed the idea with Paul Allen all summer, but something held him back.

This procrastination would lead to two years or so of Bill Gates' life that stand out for more reasons that one. At Harvard, Bill took introductory classes in law, ostensibly to become a lawyer like his father. The reason Bill wasted those two years at Harvard was because he could not stand up to his parents who pushed him towards graduate education. While no dictation was given as to what course he ought to do, Bill's parents felt that a college education would be an invaluable asset later in life. Harvard, in particular, was a prestigious university that was certain to give Bill lifelong connections in whatever career he chose.

Bill did make some very important connections at Harvard. In his sophomore year, living in Currier House, Bill met Steve Ballmer, an applied mathematics student who would later become his number two at Microsoft. In the meantime, Bill spent most of his freshman year at the Aiken Computer Center, writing code and playing games.

In the summer break of 1974, Bill decided to try and find a job. He interviewed at Honeywell and got an offer. He also put in a good word for his friend Paul, who was at that point back in Seattle working in Traf-O-Data and getting a thumping from the federal government that had recently started helping towns plan their traffic flows.

Once again, Paul and Bill were working together. The dreams of starting their own software company that had germinated a year previously were now blossoming. The computer industry was experiencing massive growth with new players joining the market every other day. There was a sense of urgency to their plans now, but still, Bill Gates held back. Allen tried his best to convince his best friend to join him in the outside, afraid that they might wait too long and miss their chance, but perhaps also a little scared to start the company alone.

One idea that was floated around was that of building a computer, but Bill vetoed it. He felt that software was the heart of computers. It was what they were better at anyways. In the end, Bill just wasn't ready to ditch school. His conflict in making a decision that seemed somewhat obvious persisted, and he returned to Harvard in the fall. It would take more than just dreams to get him to make the leap, apparently.

Back at Currier House, Bill became an avid poker player. He was, in his own words, "philosophically depressed" and trying to figure out what to do with his life. He became a full-time poker player, often playing for spells of 24 hours. When he was not at the poker table in the specially designated poker room, he would be found in the computer room, hacking away at the machine. He often slept on the tables there.

In the classroom, Bill considered becoming a

mathematician. He had always been excellent at the subject, gifted even. So good was he at math that he would often correct his lecturers at Harvard, a game of one-upmanship that he seemed to relish. Eventually, he gave up thoughts of pursuing a career in mathematics because he was not the best in school. That is how competitive Bill Gates has always been. He would much rather pull out of a competition than proceed when he was assured of being bested by someone else. And for Bill, everything in life *is* a competition.

His time in Harvard, while clearly procrastination, was not entirely in vain. He did manage to solve a pancakes puzzle that had stumped mathematicians around the country. His solution was featured in the 1979 edition of the *Discrete Mathematics* journal and was only surpassed 15 years later.

That winter, still working at Honeywell, Paul Allen came by Currier House to check on his friend. It was a visit that changed not just their lives, but also the future of the computer industry as a whole. At Harvard Square, Allen stopped to read the magazine *Popular Electronics*, a favorite of his. It was an advance copy of the momentous January 1975 magazine that carried the Altair 8080, the "World's First

Microcomputer Kit to Rival Commercial Models."

This was the break they had been looking for! Allen raced to the poker room where Bill, true to form, was engrossed in a game of poker. He recognized the significance of a personal computer in the industry. The applications would be massive. If they could create the software for the Altair, it would surely fulfill their dreams of having a computer for every home and software created by the two of them for every computer. They decided to get in touch with the makers of the Altair 8080.

The Altair 8080 was a product of Ed Roberts and his Model Instrumentation and Telemetry Systems (MITS) Company. It was built on the Intel 8080 microchip and took advantage of shrinking computer processor sizes to produce a personal computer that would be cheap enough to be bought as a house gadget. The Altair used BASIC language, but the industry had not yet created operational BASIC code that could work on the Intel chip. In its current state, the Altair 8080 was just an expensive toy that did not do much. They needed software for it.

After discussing the issue at length, Paul and Bill made a call to Ed Roberts claiming to have a BASIC program that could run on their machine. It was of at least 50 calls that MITS had received since their computer had featured in the cover of Popular Electronics. Roberts just told everyone who called to come to their offices with a functioning BASIC program.

Paul and Bill hunkered down in the computer room, working furiously to create a BASIC program for Altair. They had to do this without an Altair to test their program on, relying instead on the schematics posted along with the article announcing the release of Altair on Popular Electronics. Neither did they have the 8080 Intel microchip. Again, they had to rely on technical manuals. Displaying an incredible level of ingenuity that would later set them apart as trendsetters in the personal computer software industry, Allen wrote a program for the PDP-10 that gave it the qualities of the 8080 microchip while Bill put in all the stops to tighten the BASIC code so that it would fit into the 4k processing capacity of the Altair and still leave enough room for users to run whatever software they needed to run on the machine.

It was a grueling, eight-week ordeal that pushed the two young men to their limits as all they did was program, grab a quick bite, a wink of sleep, and then went back to programming. And they had to do all this without help from anyone except for a little known programmer by the name of Monte Davidoff, a student at Harvard who had once overhead the excited duo discussing the basic number operator subprogram. It was a fairly easy job, but none of them was eager to do it after the rigors of the main program. For the rest of the project, Davidoff ended up putting in as much time as Bill and Paul and was instrumental in helping them deliver the project on time.

However, with no formal agreement for the partnership, Monte neither received pay nor recognition. When the program was finally complete and Bill and Paul started reaping from their gamble, he simply vanished back into oblivion. Even later, when the story of Microsoft was being told and he was left out, Monte would never seek public recognition for his work.

Microsoft has been known to move the release dates for many of their products ahead after underestimating the time it would take to develop them. It is not a new problem. At the onset, Bill had promised Ed Roberts, the architect of the Altair 8080, that he would have the BASIC program ready in four weeks. The four weeks came and passed, and the two were still working on the project. In the end, the project took twice the promised amount of time.

Paul was selected to make the personal presentation at MITS offices in Albuquerque. He was excused from the last-minute operations of wrapping up loose ends of the program and given the luxury of a full night's sleep. Bill was probably a little sleep-deprived himself. He had forgotten to write a bootstrap; a program written in the 8080 machine language that enabled the Altair to load their BASIC program.

Paul wrote it at 35,000 feet on the plane ride over, giving birth to a game that he and Bill would often play, trying to outdo each other on writing the tightest loader. Bill was often the champion of these little competitions.

While Bill got his chance for a good, long sleep after eight weeks, Paul was about to come to the moment of truth. He had been disappointed that MITS was just a ragtag operation sandwiched between a Laundromat and a massage parlor. He and Bill had been thinking that their benefactor was a large and wealthy corporation. They had done the work, though, and it could not be for naught. They would go ahead with the partnership.

Back at MITS offices, Allen keyed in the loader

program and fed the tape containing BASIC into the machine. This was the first time the BASIC was operating on the Altair 8080. Not even the two programmers had seen their code at work. It worked like magic.

Even Ed Roberts had not anticipated success at the first trial. He was suitably impressed, especially considering that the program had been written on a PDP-10, not the Altair. Not only did the program work, but it could also perform the tasks other mainframe computers could do, including the Lunar Lander game very much like the one his partner had written back at Lakeside.

Bill was very excited to learn of their nifty little program's success. There'd be work to do before his brainchild could go to the market, but it was exciting to have their software on the first ever personal computer at the precipice of what he firmly believed to be a revolution in the computer industry.

But first, there were challenges to be overcome. Bill had invited Paul to the Aiken Computer Center without official approval. The school had received the PDP-10 from the US Army. The computer was still the property of the Department of Defense, intended for research into the production of hi-tech equipment for the defense forces. An argument was made that Bill and Paul's BASIC program was in part the property of Harvard because it had been produced using their equipment. The administration wanted to press for a royalty. Bill rebutted that students who wrote books using research materials from the library were not required to give royalties to the school. He was admonished for allowing Paul, an outsider, into the computer room. After that, the school started monitoring the goings-on in the computer room more keenly.

The two upstarts had done the undoable. They had managed to write software for the Altair, squeezing the bulky BASIC program into the 4k memory available on the Intel 8080 processor. It had taken them a record 8 weeks to write the basic code, then after the phenomenally successful demo at MITS, Bill and Paul, having been hounded out of the Aiken Computer Center at Harvard, used a time sharing computer to put the finishing touches on their program, fixing bugs, and getting it ready for the Altair 8080 that was soon to go to market.

In the spring of '75, Paul was offered a job by Ed Roberts to head the MITS software engineering team. He moved to Albuquerque and found himself as the sole member of the "team." Bill still could not make up his mind to drop out of school and join Allen at the frontlines of the personal computer revolution. He was fated to spend yet more time in the poker room, holding back from the future that was already happening.

The Altair 8080 was very favorably received by the public. MITS was overwhelmed with orders long before the BASIC program had been delivered to its offices by the ballsy Allen and long before their hardware department had started putting together the final product for shipping. The first kits MITS shipped out to its hungry customers came without the BASIC program Bill and Paul designed. The company then experienced the challenge of being unable to supply Altair buyers with memory for the BASIC operations.

In the midst of all the challenges that the Altair 8080 faced was Paul Allen and, a telephone call away, Bill Gates. The two had numerous phone calls, mostly about the technical difficulties Altair users faced in making their kits operable. It was becoming clearer that there existed a big market for a software company. Bill Gates' mind was finally made up. He was going to start a company with his childhood friend, all the way in Albuquerque.

His mother was horrified. She was convinced that her son was about to commit the gravest mistake of his young life, academic suicide. She set about convincing him to change his mind in characteristic Mary Gates fashion; a lunch date between her son and a colleague in the University of Washington regency, a man by the name of Samuel Stroum. Stroum was a successful entrepreneur in his own right, and like many people in the American business community, a firm believer in the rosy future of computing. Speaking later about the meeting, Stroum stated that at the end of their lunch date, the only thing he regretted having not done during the meeting was to offer to finance Bill's dream. He was convinced that not only was Bill on the right track, but also that the young man was about to make himself a fortune.

Chapter 3: Micro-Soft

Bill joined Paul at MITS and, combining the words microcomputer and software, formed a company called Micro-Soft. It was their second software company after Traf-O-Data, but it was the real thing. Bill, recognizing that, did his finest piece of negotiating yet and got Paul to agree to a 60/40 split of shares. In his opinion, he had done more to develop BASIC than Paul who had, ironically, come to him with the idea to write the program in the first place and written the loader program as well as running the first preservation.

In the strictest terms, Bill and Paul had done equal work in the development of BASIC. It may even be argued that Paul may have done a little more, having been the company's official representative at MITS. But Paul was just a good programmer. While Bill was equally as good a programmer, he was also something else; something that would set him apart from his co-founder and grant him an inordinate amount of influence and wealth in the computer industry. He was a master negotiator, a tireless competitor, and an astounding dealmaker. He obviously wanted to receive greater control of Micro-Soft than Paul. He wanted to win. He wanted to best everyone else. And he did. When it came down to it, Bill got 64% of the share to Paul's 36%.

In characteristic Maxwell fashion, Bill decided not to dig into his trust fund to finance his newly formed company. He would bootstrap it as well as possible and plow back company earnings to grow. Cheap motels and shared apartments were the way to go in the early days. Later, he would become notorious for flying economy as the chairman of a Fortune 500 company.

Micro-Soft had no offices. It was simply the legal embodiment of two extremely outstanding programmers and they still worked at MITS. Gates even joined MITS on a roadshow tour organized to drum up support for the Altair 8080. He took the opportunity of visiting numerous cities around the country to drum up interest in BASIC among members of computer club organized by MITS as another marketing gimmick. The idea paid off handsomely. The hobbyists who made up a large portion of the market for the Altair 8080 signed up in big numbers to use BASIC.

Bill also helped out with the development of 8k BASIC as well as extended 12k and 16k versions for future Altair developments with superior processing power. However, his greatest contribution to the partnership was still in the business end of it. In July 1975, the newly formed company entered into a partnership with MITS, granting MITS the universal rights to distribute BASIC in its computers. In return, Micro-Soft would earn a fixed royalty for every BASIC-equipped Altair sold and 50% of sub-license fees earned by MITS from third parties. The cunning Bill, with the guidance of his father, also stipulated that the contract would be considered null and void if MITS failed to "use its best efforts to ... promote (BASIC)." It was a piece of foresight that would later save the duet's efforts to create BASIC.

Bill and Paul were soon overwhelmed with their programming work at MITS. As the only two programmers serving a market of thousands, it was impossible to keep up with the workload. It was time to call in the cavalry. From Lakeside, Bill recruited Chris Larson, a passionate teenager who had succeeded Bill as the programming whiz in charge of the school's computerized class schedule. While Bill had given his senior class Friday afternoon off (and become a hero), Larson had put himself in a classroom full of girls (and become a legend). The second recruitment was of Monte Davidoff, the unsung hero who had helped him and Paul complete the BASIC program for Altair back in Harvard.

The four would revert to the familiar "hardcore" lifestyle of coding into the night, sleeping every which way, and eating fries and Coke. Ed disapproved of this lifestyle, especially their preference for metal rock 'n' roll. He was more of a country music man, preferring its smooth flow to the hard sounds of rock. In deference to their employer, Bill and his group would not listen to their preferred music while Roberts was in the office. But as soon as he was out of the door, they would be blasting away.

There was another source of friction between Bill and Ed. As a natural-born entrepreneur with a keen sense for business, Bill could not stand the half-assed way of project delivery of MITS. He thought everything was a mess, and he was not huge on Ed's style of leadership. That would have been all very well if Bill had not kept it to himself. Plenty of other people thought the same, but they kept out of it, probably because they felt it was not their place to voice their thoughts. Well, not Bill.

In addition to clashing with Ed Roberts about every other topic under the surface of the earth- Hiroshima and Nagasaki among others- Bill argued with his boss-partner about his running of MITS. He was firmly convinced that the operations of MITS concerned him because his company could only make money on the back of Altair, but Roberts would be hard pressed to see it that way. In his opinion, which was voiced loudly and often, Bill was too confrontational for his own good and he should focus on writing code, which he was excellent at.

All through 1975, Bill, Larson, and Davidoff shuttled between their respective schools and MITS, leaving Paul to work software at MITS all on his own. He got along okay with Roberts, much better than Bill, possibly because he was less outspoken, and business minded. He displayed a rare breed of business vision by foreseeing the need for a floppy disk-storage system for the Altair 8080 and tasking Bill with developing the BASIC software for the program. Bill procrastinated until MITS asked Paul to write the program, then he wrote the code on a yellow legal pad and, five days later, emerged from the MITS software lab with the DISK BASIC program.

Now the Altair 8080 was not an easy machine to operate. MITS took an awfully long time to deliver, and after taking ownership of the machine, buyers had to figure out how to put it together and there was no assurance that it would actually work. Few of them ever gave a thought to the creators of the BASIC software that allowed them to perform the limited functions the computer could execute. The BASIC software was soon a hot commodity, and hobbyists took it from whatever avenues they could, often from other hobbyists who had gotten it from other hobbyists. Microsoft was losing money because Altair 8080 users were virtually stealing their life's work. Bill Gates could not stand the effrontery.

In February 1976, Bill wrote an article in the Altair newsletter in which he made a stinging admonition of hobbyists who copied BASIC rather than buying from authorized dealers from which Microsoft could earn royalties. Convinced that this sort of piracy was the reason why Microsoft was not making any money, Bill took it upon himself to ensure that the company got its fair share of monetary gain for their investment. The article was titled "An Open Letter to Hobbyists" and it would generate for its author widespread notoriety in computer circles all over the country. With this one article, Bill Gates made himself famous, but rather unpopular for taking the lead as the advocate for a fair wage for a fair day's work through the mainstream sale of software.

Not everyone agreed with his views. Hobbyists around the country were up in an uproar. The straight shooting Bill had called them "thieves" in no uncertain terms and accused them of undermining the very people who made it possible for them to enjoy the wonders of personal computers, programmers. Among other arguments, Bill asserted that his company needed the royalties from the sale of BASIC to hire programmers and produce better software for hobbyists. No one could afford to spend hours, accrue tens of thousands in computer time, and make no money out of it. It would not be a sustainable business. It was a very impassioned argument, but some of it rubbed people off the wrong way.

The Southern California Computer Society threatened a suit for defamation, claiming that Bill Gates had branded them all as thieves. Everyone was indignant, even those who had pirated their BASIC. Some felt very justified in doing this, arguing that because BASIC had been written using computer facilities of Harvard College, it had been paid for using taxpayer money and was thus open source.

Bill Gates could hear none of it. After his open letter to hobbyists had started the debate, he pursued the matter further at the World Altair

Computer Convention in March of 76, reiterating his previous remarks and maintaining that hobbyists were ripping off his innovation. Although some people sympathized with his views, they were in the minority.

The issue of BASIC piracy was turning out to be a public relations nightmare not just for Microsoft, but also for MITS. In fact, MITS, as the umbrella company from which then little-known Microsoft was operating, was suffering more. Hundreds of companies had come up with their own version of the personal computer in the one year since the Altair 8080 had graced the cover of *Popular Electronics*. The company was further compromised by the fact that Bill had typed his letter on MITS stationery. There was no way for the company to distance itself from views that a growing number of people were starting to consider scandalous.

Ed Roberts was upset. He demanded that Gates set the record straight and surprisingly, the combative Bill Gates recognized his mistake in using MITS stationery and agreed to write a second letter. This ability to be fervently convinced of one thing and change his mind upon receiving evidence to the contrary would set Bill Gates apart as a world-class leader in the future. His ego was not too big to admit to the truth.

In "A Second and Final Letter," still in the Altair newsletter, Bill stuck mostly to his guns, welcoming discussion on the issue of computer software. He amended by clarifying that his first letter was not an indictment of all hobbyists, only of those who acquired BASIC software through illicit channels such as through unlicensed second-hand sellers and blatant illicit copying.

The pirating had helped spread BASIC to all parts of the country. Bill Gates' indictment of illicit users of the program, and the resultant scandal, propelled him to fame above and beyond his co-founder.

As more and more computer manufacturers started sourcing their software from Microsoft, the company gained prominence as the leader in software development for microcomputers.

Between launching a one-man crusade against piracy, running Microsoft and writing code, Bill was increasingly missing out on his education. However, like the skilled businessman, Bill was careful to hedge his bets. Even after forming Micro-Soft, he preferred to defer rather than annulling his course completely. In the event that his dream did not pan out, there would always be Harvard to fall back on. It was an unnecessary insurance plan. He finally dropped out in early 1977 to focus on his rapidly growing software company.

In the later years of Microsoft starting out, Bill Gates would be identified with a group of young, oft-considered fanatical, programmers at Microsoft. These young people were gathered over a couple of years, starting with Marc McDonald in 1976, followed by Steve Wood and Albert Chu. Former schoolmates Chris Larson and Richard Wieland came and went, until the latter finally left for good and the former stayed for good after finishing high school. The company also opened its first offices in 1976. It was now firmly on the path to massive growth.

In its new offices, Microsoft set about developing new products, including a FORTRAN equivalent of BASIC for the Intel 8080 chip. The initiative of figuring out what direction the industry was taking and positioning Microsoft accordingly, rested squarely on Bill as the manager, and he executed his duties perfectly.

With his old "call everyone until someone agrees to buys something from you" style of marketing developed with the Lakeside

Programmers Group and Traf-O-Data, Bill landed the two most lucrative clients Microsoft had ever had up to that time; General Electric and the National Cash Register. For the NCR, Microsoft wrote what would be known as the Standalone Disk BASIC for NCR.

There was a lot of money to be made from the ballooning number of microcomputer producing companies, but Microsoft was hindered by its legal and financial connection to MITS. Ed Roberts took pleasure in exercising his veto powers over whom Microsoft could sell BASIC to, a result of which meant that the company lost a lot of business with companies that were competing with MITS for the microcomputer market.

MITS owed much of its phenomenal success to the BASIC program on its computer, and in extension to Microsoft and Bill and Paul for continued development and refinement of the software. Ed Roberts, the hulking manager of the company, knew that he could not afford to antagonize Bill Gates. His company would suffer if Microsoft withdrew its technical support for the BASIC programs that its computers run on. The two were unequaled in the software industry. He could not, however, allow his competitors to get their hands on the secret to his continued dominance of the industry.

Bill Gates was growing increasingly frustrated with Ed Roberts for what he felt was an iron grasp on the feet of Microsoft keeping the company from capitalizing on the popularity of its BASIC program. Ed's stubborn hold on the company and his eagerness to use the powers granted to his company in the licensing contract deal from two years before, created a lot of friction between the two men. Bill could approach a computer maker and convince them to use BASIC language on their computers, negotiate a deal to supply the program, only to have the deal struck down with little ceremony, by Ed Roberts.

Some of the companies that Microsoft was forbade by MITS to do business with included Zilog, Rand, Courier, Isyx, Control Data, Lexar, Delta Data, Astro, Lawrence Livermore, Rydacom, Magnavox, and ADDS. This was after a whole year of Gates' classic brand of salesmanship that involved badgering, persuasion, and negotiation till the companies were convinced by his ironclad determination that BASIC would become the industry standard. Another company, Intelligence Systems Corporation, approached MITS for a license agreement, but the latter quoted a price so high that Intelligent Systems had to pull out of the deal.

As though Bill was not already pissed off enough about losing what would have been in upwards of $100,000, Ed wrote to Microsoft with a terse reminder to his right to dictate sublicenses of BASIC and forbade Bill and Paul from contacting any other third party to discuss licensing deals until the issue was resolved.

In essence, Ed was simply flexing his muscles, relying on the licensing agreement his company had signed with Microsoft giving it universal rights to distribute BASIC. The company was well-off selling the Altair 8080 and a few other computer models and variations, but Microsoft, as a software company exclusively, was at a loss. It could not hope to grow if MITS was controlling their purse strings.

Even more alarming, the company had so far made about $180,000 in royalties from the sale of BASIC through MITS, the capacity placed on royalties in their deal. They would soon be without a revenue stream, and for a young business, it would be catastrophic. MITS remained unconcerned to the plight of Microsoft. Perhaps Ed Roberts, after years of quibbling with Bill Gates, felt that he had found his opportunity to strike back and hurt his outspoken critic where it hurt the most. Perhaps he was just a businessman concerned only with his company and meant Microsoft no harm. What is clearly apparent, however, is that Bill Gates learned from this incident to enforce contracts to the letter, even when they hurt partners. Later, as a benefactor to the software industry, the company would reflect the very qualities that their very first benefactor had used to almost smother its growth and crush its spirit.

Falling back on his father for a little legal advice, Bill issued a letter to MITS terminating the agreement between the two companies. They accused the company of failing to promote BASIC as agreed and flippantly issuing third-party licenses. The letter seemed to do the trick, but Roberts would file a motion at the Bernalillo County District Court restraining Microsoft from issuing licenses to third parties themselves after learning that Microsoft was about to sign a licensing deal with Texas Instruments, a bitter rival that had almost driven MITS out of business and forced it to move from calculators-its former area of business- into microcomputers.

As the legal battle was just warming up and Microsoft was suffering through its worst fiscal year ever, MITS received a buyout bid from Pertec. The Pertec legal team met with Bill and dismissed him based on his scraggy appearance. He proved himself equal to the whole team in shouting matches and in a game of wits. Ultimately, Microsoft sailed through on the case based on the mistakes of Pertec. In blatant disregard to the significance of the "best efforts" provision of the agreement signed between MITS and Microsoft, Pertec wrote to Microsoft, informing them that the company no longer intended to promote BASIC or license to other microcomputer companies as they were all competitors.

The case went all the way to an arbitration hearing, pitting the giant corporation against the very young Microsoft. A lot was at stake, but the arbitrator was finding it difficult to understand the highly technical terms of the agreement. In the end, the arbitrator made a ruling based on the legality of the terms of the contract. BASIC was a Microsoft product and the company ought to have the right to market and distribute it in the best interests of the company. Microsoft historians agree that were Microsoft to have lost that case, it would have been a fatal blow that none of its founders would have overcome.

After the legal victory, Microsoft went to work filling the backlog of customers that had accumulated on the course of the trial. And in the mind of Microsoft's founder and business manager, it was clear that the company would have to be very careful who it went to bed with and the terms of their partnership. Bill Gates was shaping out to be an incredibly clever businessman and gifted deal maker. He was also growing very good at programming after years of practice, but he would soon be too busy managing the growing company to do much in the way of programming.

If the story of Bill Gates may sometimes read like the history of Microsoft that might be because, more than anyone else, Bill Gates shaped the world's largest computer software company with more than four decades at its head. Paul Allen was a co-founder, but he remained mostly on the software development end of operations before leaving in 1983, less than a decade after he and Bill registered Micro-Soft.

It was Bill who shaped the culture of Microsoft through hiring, and through decision-making on product development. He made the deals, oversaw the writing of software, and often edited it. Bill Gates poured his heart and soul into Microsoft since he was 19, making it his whole life, scorning anyone at Microsoft who did not exhibit his passion for work. Bill Gates made Microsoft his life, unequivocally and uninhibitedly, and the company naturally became as close to a corporate clone of him as one company can get to its founder. Few other founders can be attributed to such great influence on their corporeal creations as Bill Gates. The influence Bill Gates had on programmers who worked at Microsoft is undeniably huge. He controlled the business side of the company and influenced product development for every iconic Microsoft product. His life's history and that of Microsoft is indeed one and the same.

The more abrasive style of Microsoft's competitive culture cannot surely be attributed to anyone but Bill Gates. Everyone who has ever interacted with the Gates and Allen, from classmates and teachers, to business partners, attest to Bill's competitive and assertiveness, to the point of being aggressive, and Paul Allen's sociability and affable nature. For a lot of people, Bill came across as being superior and aloof, the kind of person who would not hesitate to call someone out when they were being 'stupid' or making his thoughts, however critical they might be, known.

A case in point is the aftermath of the trial with Pertec. Years later, Ed Roberts singled Bill out as the conniving one of the duo while praising Paul as a respectable person. He may be partial to Paul for their years at MITS and prejudiced against Bill Gates for besting him in a high stakes game involving highly valuable software, but his sentiments follow a pattern that indicates the competitiveness of Bill Gates rubbing people the wrong way, and him, focused solely on Microsoft and its dominance of the computer software industry, not caring. His singular drive towards success and winning would prove to be his greatest asset and also the biggest source of grief for him and his legacy, Microsoft.

Chapter 4: Microsoft Explodes

After winning back the rights to market and distribute BASIC, Microsoft experienced a period of explosive growth starting in 1978. Free from the shackles of MITS and Ed Roberts, Bill Gates led the company into a period of diversification, creating new versions of BASIC for new microchips (other than the Intel 8080 microchip) and also writing programs on the COBOL language as well as FORTRAN. Bill allowed his group of programming warriors to retain their individuality around the office with no official dress code.

The most important things at Microsoft have always been to work harder than competitors, create superior products, and emerge as the leader in their market. The corporate culture of Microsoft in the early years was very informal. Other than having a very young labor force and creating a relaxed working environment, the company, including its supremo Bill Gates, took to a lot of fraternity activities, like sneaking into a construction site at night and racing the heavy equipment or racing their cars on the freeway at the dead of night. These activities were perhaps a natural way to let off steam after coding for the whole day and half the night. With their work-hard-and-play-harder style, Microsoft programmers, led by Bill Gates, would go ahead to conquer the computer software industry and have a load of fun while at it. The company was doing well, growing organically with no debt, transcending their sales year on year, and making a good profit. While Bill was not wasteful or extravagant in any way, the security of running a company that was very profitable and obviously heading towards greater profitability gave Bill a period of carefree living that he could not replicate later as the profile of the company grew. Street racing was a favorite pastime of his, going as high as 80 mph in stretches of road designated for 35. It is from these times that the iconic mugshot of Bill Gates when he was arrested for over speeding was taken.

But that is not to say that Bill was all fun and games. He was a demanding, sometimes confrontational boss who would always be pushing his programmers to do more, faster, and better. What's more, Bill expected his employees to be as demanding of him as he was of them. Those people who could go head-to-head with him in an argument and not back down from a confrontation when they believed in what they were talking about, would become a favorite of Bill. He always liked people who could stand up for themselves and even stand up to him.

Bill, always with a keen sense of market direction, targeted the Original Equipment Manufacturer (OEM) companies by creating utility to their products. He was convinced they would take both the personal computer companies and software companies like Microsoft to new heights. His skills as a salesman saw Microsoft software get into all sorts of computerized operations, from hospital imaging devices to air traffic control and others. In the meantime, Paul took the lead programming department, ensuring that contracts signed by Bill on behalf of Microsoft were properly delivered.

Bill learned from his narrow escape from a crushing defeat under Pertec how detrimental a contract could be. Getting the deal was not the only important thing. It was critical to write the right kind of contract and protect the company from possible harm in the hands of their partners. Always eager to save the company expensive overhead costs, Bill learned the legal language of computers and wrote some of the contracts himself rather than hire a lawyer.

By far the most brilliant bit of business that Bill

Gates did was to pursue a new dimension of expansion for Microsoft into Japan. The year was 1977, and Microsoft had a dozen or so competitors in America. He had visited Japan before and was impressed by the amount of research that went on there. He was quite sure that the Asian country would be the growth region of the near future, and he set about positioning Microsoft to reap the benefits. Moving into the Japanese market also ensured that he could service the software needs of computer hardware companies that were coming up and not leave a void that would obviously be filed by a future competitor.

Bill Gates' push to enter the Japan market was boosted by the business smarts of a Japanese techpreneur named Kazuhiko Nishi who had made his entry into the computer industry producing a computer magazine. Having made numerous valuable connections in the nascent computer industry, Nishi spotted the opportunity to make money by supplying computer manufacturers in Japan with software.

Bill and Nishi met at the 1977 National Computer Conference which was held in Dallas in that year. Scheduled as a one-hour business meeting, their introduction ended up stretching into an eight-hour conversation, with the two bonding over their mutual high hope for personal computers in the world. Bill Gates made an agreement making Kazuhiko Microsoft's agent in the Far East on behalf of the company.

While the deal with Kazuhiko was ironed out with little complications and would turn out to be one of Microsoft's most profitable, Bill was not always a great negotiator. Some of his negotiation tactics have been criticized as being too aggressive, described once as "pushing customers and potential business partners till they go along with his proposal" rather than bargaining till they reached a deal both could be happy with. The arm twisting would turn to anger when he could not get his way, which often lost the company some great deals after the other party felt pushed too far. This occurred once with a subsidiary for the Intel Corporation.

Bill was definitely under a lot of pressure, what with his responsibility as the business manager for Microsoft and his insistence on putting in his hours in the programming lab. But the company was located too far away from everybody else. Executives visiting Microsoft to do business with Bill would have to fly long distances, and Bill also had to spend days on the road simply to meet potential partners and make deals. The company had been registered in Albuquerque because MITS was located there and they had been the main (and only) source of income. The Silicon Valley was picking up the pace as the location for companies in the growing tech industry, but Bill and Allen felt that Seattle, their hometown, might be a more suitable location. They had both grown rather homesick. The company would go back home in 1978.

As Microsoft settled down in its new Seattle office located in the old National Bank in 1979, Bill Gates made a decision that would have an everlasting impact on the future of the company down the line. A few months prior, Intel had come up with the 8086 chip, an upgrade from the 8080 that had sired the personal computer industry. While the rest of the industry stuck to the 8080 chip, Bill and co-founder Paul Allen chose instead to create a BASIC interpreter program for the new microchip. The 8086 chip had one advantage over the 8080. Intel had made it specifically for the microcomputer. It was a giant leap forward, introducing 16-bit that had the capability to process much more complicated programs than the 8080.

When Gates attended the 1979 National Computer Conference in New York City, he had the enormous pleasure of showing off the 8086 BASIC operating on a Seattle Computers Central Processing Unit. Seattle Computers was the only computer manufacturer to have incorporated the 8086 chip into a CPU board at the time. The Microsoft-Seattle Computers setup faced stiff competition for publicity from the Apple II computer. The 8086 BASIC was not nearly as exciting as VisiCalc, futuristic electronic spreadsheet software that ran on Apple II. VisiCalc was the brainchild of a Philadelphia born computer scientist from Massachusetts Institute of Technology (MIT).

Another company would one-up Bill gates before he decided to start a consumer products division to compete in the profitable utility programs market. The personal computer was slowly finding its footing in the business world after all, replacing books, ledgers, and huge libraries by providing a faster, more effective way of performing common office functions like bookkeeping. The company was MicroPro, and it had come up with WordStar, the world's first word processing software.

His 8086 BASIC was a rather narrow undertaking, following in the footsteps of previous BASIC for the 8080. Bill Gates now recognized that utility software, not computer language, would be the future of programming. If Microsoft was to have a hope of competing with these new entrants, it would have to think bigger.

The man Bill Gates put to head the new consumer software division had first come to his attention in 1978 as one of the pirates selling his Altair BASIC with no license. His name was Vern Raburn. The two bonded over their love for racing, and while Raburn did not match Bill's competitive streak on the race track, he was a charismatic man who raced to win. He was the perfect man to head the division Bill gates knew would represent the future of Microsoft.

As Microsoft continued on its upwards growth, it started making recruitments in the business section rather than just bringing in programmers. Bill Gates could no longer run the company singlehandedly as he had done in the formative years. These new hires often thought they were coming into a tech company run by programming nerds who did not know a thing about business, but they were in for a rude shock. The company's first marketing director, Steve Smith, was one such employee. Not only was he a well-learned business administrator, but he had also worked with some of the biggest businesses in America at the time. Thinking he would bring a new age of "effective" management to the apparently disorganized company, he found himself getting schooled by Bill Gates on the speedy execution of contracts.

Bill Gates made his personal conviction the mantra of Microsoft; "A computer on every desk and Microsoft software in every computer." All negotiations and business decisions were made with this goal in mind. The passion and conviction with which Bill Gates sold Microsoft's customers (the manufacturers of personal computers) on this ideal helped the company retain their trust and confidence even when they were running late in delivering on a contracted piece of work. In rare cases, he would even sell an executive, who'd come to protest delays on some programming, a new one! But sometimes he promised too much and was unable to deliver. Working with IMSAI Manufacturing in 1978, he had signed a contract to produce an overlay editor; a nifty little program that allowed the bulky FORTRAN language to be divided into smaller, easier to process units, an important feature at a time when 8 kb memory chips were the norm. Bill was only saved paying hefty penalties stipulated in the contract because IMSAI went out of business before it could collect on them.

Now, it might come as a surprise that what Microsoft was selling at the onset was not operating systems. In the current world, Windows is the most popular OS and may even be considered to be synonymous to Microsoft. But BASIC was simply a computer language, the baseline on which operating systems are built. Utility software is then built on top of the operating system, creating a three-tiered system of software. In 1979, the BASIC interpreter was the standard computer language for personal computers. The Control Program for Microcomputers (CP/M) operating system developed by Digital Research was as close to a standard OS as the personal computer industry had at the time.

It was not until 1980 that Bill Gates engineered the entry of Microsoft into the operating systems market with a license from AT&T to repackage its UNIX operating system as XENIX, making the OS cutting edge by adopting it for the 16-bit 8086 microprocessor. Ironically, the one product that Microsoft pioneered, computer language, would become its least recognized contribution to the personal computer in later years, overtaken several times over by the Windows OS and Microsoft's suite of software like Word, Publisher, Internet Explorer, etc.

About 800 miles away in Palo Alto, California, another tech visionary was making waves in the personal computer industry. Having started with an ingenious idea to use a purchase order by *The Byte* computer shop to acquire the components for his friend Steve Wozniak's invention from Cramer Electronics, Steve Jobs had quickly built a fledgling computer company from the garage of his parent's house. Steve Jobs did not believe in conformity, so while the rest of the personal computer industry incorporated the Intel 8080 microchip in their processing units, Apple computer used a different manufacturer altogether. The MOS Technology 6502 microchip would be their processor of choice. Their OS was also proprietary and was a closely guarded secret. Computer users seemed to appreciate the novelty of Apple.

The company's computers were selling better than any other personal computer in the market. In fact, the only part of Apple's core architecture that was outsourced was the computer language for the Apple II Plus when Wozniak's Integer BASIC was replaced with a

Microsoft BASIC variation named Applesoft BASIC. The partnership with Apple was not something Bill took for granted. There was a big current market for Apple software, and the seasoned businessman could tell that Apple's products would grow even more popular, creating an even bigger market. There was just one challenge, and it was almost insurmountable. It was not a problem for Microsoft alone either, but one that every software company would face in trying to sell to Apple users. The OS and processors were not complimentary.

It was Paul Allen who would come up with the solution to this problem in one brainstorming session at the Microsoft parking lot. Rather than attempt to convert all the code into 6502 compatible versions, Microsoft would make a smart card that allowed Apple computers to run CP/M software. It was a solution for the whole CP/M and 8080 Intel processor computer software industry, and it proved to be quite successful. The nifty little device would be named the SoftCard, and it would end up bringing to Microsoft the life-changing deal that propelled it to its current heights.

Bill Gates and Microsoft were leading the pack in computer technology, making industry-wide innovations that greatly boosted the growth of software for the personal computer industry. It would take Microsoft a single partnership to explode into the gargantuan software company it has become today, but before that, a legendary hire had to be made.

Bill was young, unmarried, and singularly dedicated to Microsoft. He expected all his employees to demonstrate the same commitment to work as he did, which made Microsoft a rather uncomfortable place to work for the older employees who had families and who preferred a healthier work-life balance. Steve Wood, the Microsoft general manager from 1977 to 1980, left with his wife in part because he felt Microsoft's intense work culture did not suit him. Steve Wood had been part of the programming team as well as performing his duties as a general manager in a company that had 30 employees and 28 programmers. Counting Bill Gates as proficient in computer programming, the only Microsoft employee with no programming skills was the secretary.

Bill Gates filled the open position with an old friend from the Harvard Currier House who knew very little about programming and a lot about business, Steve Ballmer. A new position, president's assistant, was created for him. It was somewhat of an ambiguous position, but Ballmer filled it with grace and eagerness, performing whatever task Bill Gates assigned to him. It is likely that no one at the time knew, but Bill Gates had just made the appointment that completed his team perfectly. The new assistant to the president had another qualification that set him apart from most of the senior employees at Microsoft: he could achieve what Bill Gates called high bandwidth communication. In essence, he was not beyond getting into a shouting match with the boss to argue a point.

Chapter 5: IBM

Once you have started pursuing your interests in real earnest, you may face opposition. Resistance comes to test the ambitious. But there is always that one event or series of events that create a turning point, propelling you to heights unimagined, even by yourself, before.

Bill Gates and his brainchild (Microsoft) did not really gain prominence in the industry until he went into business with the International Business Machines (IBM). IBM had made the first entry into computers in the 1950s, but until 1978, it had viewed the personal computer revolution as a passing fad. When it became clear that the market was shifting towards personal computers and the company might lose its foothold on the computer market, the IBM Corporate Management Committee hastened to authorize their engineers to create a personal computer.

They would have to resort to sourcing for many of the computer's components from third parties, including the operating system and computer language. Moreover, the company, afraid of playing catch-up with Apple if it delayed for too long coming up with its PC, gave the engineering team just one year to get the IBM PC to the market. The responsibility of obtaining the operating system was given to Jack Sams, a programming and operating systems technician who admired Bill Gates' work at Microsoft and wrongly believed Microsoft to be the architect of CP/M because of the recently released SoftCard. Even though Microsoft's XENIX OS was far from the industry standard, Sams considered Microsoft before looking into Digital Research, the architects of CP/M.

The IBM engineering team envisioned a computer that would appeal to the masses. The CP/M operating system was the closest thing to an industry standard on which most proprietary software ran back then. Bill Gates had to reorganize his calendar, canceling a scheduled meeting with a potential client, when he received the call informing his office of IBM's impending visit. The logistics the meeting were handled by Bill Gates with the assistance of Steve Ballmer, the latter having found a role he could actively fill at Microsoft after a short period of occupying a rather ambiguous job description.

Bill was faced with a bit of a catch-22 situation.

Making a deal with IBM to supply BASIC for their personal computer would be huge for Microsoft. The only operating system license Bill had was the XENIX one from AT&T, and he did not share a cordial enough relationship to recommend them to Big Blue. But it was imperative that he take care of IBM's OS problem, because chances were if the company representatives made a deal with another OS manufacturer, they might procure BASIC from them too. While Microsoft BASIC was an industry standard at this point, there were still other companies that dealt in computer languages. Also, if IBM could not outsource the software for their PC, there was a chance they would resort to creating proprietary software themselves like Apple. Bill Gates had just one option; help IBM find a reliable OS, or his BASIC deal would be off too.

The CP/M was slowly gaining prominence as somewhat of an industry standard in operating systems at this point. A lot of the applications software that was being written operated on the CP/M OS and if the company played their cards well, they had a shot at total domination of the OS industry. CP/M was made by Digital Research, a software company owned by a man named Gary Kildall. Gary had done business with Bill before; Microsoft was a CP/M licensee who had most remarkably created the SoftCard and used the CP/M OS to allow Apple users to run CP/M programs. Gary and Bill were friendly competitors. Bill was keeping Microsoft mostly off operating systems and Gary kept off computer language through an unspoken no-competition agreement.

Knowing that Gary was better placed to fulfill IBM's operating system needs (all they had to do was license CP/M to them), Bill sent Jack Sims and his team to the Digital Research Institute offices. That he would supply the BASIC program was an ironclad assurance as long as DRI made the operating system. It was a pretty easy arrangement, except it wasn't. The events that transpired during Jack Sims' trip to DRI remain to be hotly contested, but Gary happened to be out of the office at this crucial point, and the IBM delegate was kept waiting for a while by Gary's wife who was running the office at the time. Gary Kildall could not cut a vacation short to oversee what had the potential to be the biggest deal of his life. Another failing on DRI's part would eventually hand the IBM operating system project to Bill on a silver platter.

IBM was an old-fashioned sort of company, a sprawling corporation that had numerous levels of management and channels of accountability. Secrecy and security was a very important aspect of their dealings with any outside partners. Bill had to sign a non-disclosure agreement to even discuss the upcoming personal computer project. Digital Research Institute was not as well-informed or as graceful as Bill. Gary's wife and a DRI lawyer would not sign the non-disclosure agreement; ostensibly because it gave IBM an unfair advantage to use confidential information disclosed at the meeting and barred DRI from taking the same liberty. The two were dreadfully deadlocked. The first day of their dealings ended with no discussions opened and both sides deeply frustrated. A little later, Jack Sims talked to Gary Kildall himself. IBM was still interested in arriving at an agreement with DRI. The former just had to consent to come up with a 16-bit OS in the limited time the IBM engineering department had been given to make the PC. But Gary, the head of DRI, was unwilling to commit DRI resources to the terms of the proposed deal. *"Sorry IBM, what you are asking for is just too much."* The deal fell through.

Jack Sims knew he could count on one person to produce an operating system in the limited time IBM needed it. Bill Gates was still a hardcore programmer, even though now he was more likely to be found haggling with clients on the executive desk rather than slumped on a table in the programming room after a whole night of programming. He still did all these of things, but he was increasingly moving away from the more technical side of Microsoft and focusing more on the business end of things. His team of handpicked programmers more than made up for his absence in the programming lab. Bill was the only person who could appreciate the immense opportunity it was to produce the OS for IBM's upcoming personal computer. He was also the kind of man who would take all the concerns that IBM had regarding the operating system and make them his, solving each and every one of them. Microsoft was put back in the project.

Richard Branson, the head of the Virgin Group of Companies, is often credited with coining the quote; "If someone asks you to do something you don't know how to do, say yes. Then figure out how to do it later." Bill Gates' life is the epitome of this philosophy. A prominent software manufacturer had just turned down a lucrative project to do business with what was the world's biggest computer manufacturer because there was no time to upgrade their 8-bit CP/M to the 16-bit platform. DRI was a company with a broad spectrum of experience creating operating systems while Microsoft had zero experience in that area. Bill signed between the dotted lines and then resorted to figuring out how to deliver the project later, and history rewarded him with a legacy to rival that of any modern businessman.

It turned out that Bill didn't even have to make his band of programming geniuses write the software that would be used in IBM PCs. A 16-bit operating system was currently being vended by Seattle Computer Products right in their city. The operating system was aptly named 86-QDOS, a numerical reference to the 8086 Intel microchip and an acronym of a quick and dirty operating system (QDOS). Having worked with Seattle Computer Products in the 1979 National Computer Conference in New York City, the two were already in a supportive partnership. In a bit of excellent business machination, Bill approached Seattle Computers with a deal; $25,000 in exchange for their 86-QDOS and a free licensing deal to use the operating system in their computers. It would have been close to impossible to work on an operating system from scratch and create the BASIC programs within the one year IBM had given them. Bill's crafty business sense saved Microsoft more than one year's work. With every base covered and Bill having a good idea how to deliver the 16-bit operating system IBM needed, Bill had to travel all the way to Boca Raton to discuss his ideas with IBM and negotiate the IBM-Microsoft partnership.

In negotiations, Bill made another genius decision that contributed greatly to Microsoft's future dominance of the PC software industry. After acquiring an operational OS from Seattle Computers, Microsoft planned to refine it and produce a slightly different operating system. So far, the PC industry had outstanding computer makers like Apple, but not a behemoth the size and influence of IBM. Bill expected that IBM's market smarts and promotional acumen would further expand the market. The fact that IBM, unlike best-selling PC-maker of the time (Apple), planned to use externally sourced computer parts also created the possibility of other PC-makers cloning the IBM PC. These computers would also need operating systems and BASIC programs, meaning that there was a chance of Microsoft's market also expanding. Microsoft needed to retain the rights to their software if they were to capitalize on this market. Luckily, IBM never intended to take ownership of the software that went into their computer. Microsoft was obligated to develop and provide support for all programs they would make for the IBM PC. This would turn out to be the best thing to ever happen to Bill Gates and Microsoft.

Bill was on point in all negotiations with IBM concerning the software side of their upcoming PC. He brought Steve Ballmer and another Microsoft employee Bob O'Rear as backups, but Paul Allen, the co-founder of Microsoft, was left behind. Paul's role in Microsoft's future was increasingly being overshadowed by Bill's somewhat overbearing leadership. He was focused on the technical operations of the company, and as the business maneuverings of the company received greater media attention than the back-end ops, Bill inevitably received greater credit for Microsoft. Soon, Paul wouldn't be around to run even the programming operations of Microsoft. Bill's endeavor to win the IBM project was further bolstered by a rapport that developed between him and an eccentric IBM executive named Don Estridge. The two connected on their mutual conviction that computers were the future of the world. It was also Don who would disclose to Bill that the IBM CEO John Opel, like Bill's mother, was a president of United Way. Moreover, the two had served together on the national board. Although the fact is not verifiable, prominent leaders of the partnership on the IBM side like Jack Sims were quite sure that their boss had been convinced to take a chance on the 24 years-old Bill in part because he was well acquainted with his mother.

Three months had passed since the IBM Corporate Management Committee had ordered Jack Sims to have a computer ready to ship in one year. The next nine months would be brutal for Bill Gates, just as they were for all Microsoft employees, as they raced to deliver two critical bits of software (the BASIC and OS) that would obviously be scrutinized nationwide and heavily impact the company's future. Don Estridge, not Jack Sims, was now IBM's chief project manager of the PC, which the company had codenamed "Project Chess".

Bill Gates' life was at this point dominated by his responsibilities as the president of the then million-dollar company. He worked sixteen hour days and travelled the world promoting Microsoft products. His biggest social indulgence was the occasional workplace party thrown by his employees, a drive in the deserted Seattle streets in the middle of the night to calm his nerves and think, and Sunday night dinners at his parents' home. The rest of the office would take Thursday night off to bond over foosball, their mutual fascination with science fiction, and a few drinks. Bill, too busy running

Microsoft, could not spare the time. Not even his closest friends were allowed to encroach on his schedule, especially on social occasions. Bill's friendship with Carl Edmark, a boyhood friend, unraveled in 1983 because the latter was late for a movie date. His focus on Microsoft was such that he could not afford to waste any time at all.

When he started working on the IBM project, Bill warned his parents that he might not make it to the Sunday night dinners or any other family events for a few months. His prediction would turn out to be prophetic, because it would be more than six months before Bill attended another dinner at his parents' house.

Bill Gates had been raised in a very close-knit family. He loved his parents and enjoyed the family dinners immensely. But he was willing to sacrifice the indulgence to dedicate himself completely and immerse all his energies on a project he knew would propel him and his company to great heights. This willingness to sacrifice and the drive to do everything he needed to do to win was trademark Bill Gates. While a company that specialized in operating systems wouldn't go out of its way to make a modification from 8-bit to 16-bit for the sake of a lucrative deal, Bill accepted, figured out a way to acquire the necessary infrastructure to create the operating system, found an operating system that he would need minimal work to customize to the IBM PC, then thrust himself into the task of ensuring that he delivered with gusto.

For the one year that the IBM project occupied the time of practically every employee at Microsoft, Bill Gates was not giving up much of a social life. Even though he didn't seem to care, he was doubtlessly a millionaire at the time, running a multi-million company. He was also smart, passionate, and while he was no underwear model, Bill Gates had enough appeal to have a really lively dating life. Sure he was a bit of a nerd, a little socially awkward, and given to impress people more with his arrogance than his personal charm, but Bill was still quite a catch. However, while the likes of Paul and Wood and other Microsoft employees were settled with young families, Bill Gates remained stubbornly single. He did not even follow the route taken by his good friend and confidante Kay Nishi- that of womanizing; in fact, he considered Kay's ways quite unacceptable.

The only indication that Bill Gates was once a young hot-blooded male with a healthy sexual appetite comes from the maker of the Osborne computer, Adam Osborne. A proper English fellow who rather admired Bill, he spoke of a time when Bill had an affair with an executive in his company then told him off when Osborne warned him to stop the conduct. Quoted by James Wallace and Jim Erickson, an Osborne executive stated that Bill had a thing for older women back then. Well, it is good to know that he did outgrow the fondness.

Bill Gates' work in the IBM project was to supervise the programming team and run interference with the IBM supervisors. In the nine months the Microsoft programming team worked around the clock writing code for the 86-QDOS, Bill made numerous trips to Boca Raton. He also personally looked over every line of code written by his programming team, sometimes making a change here and there. The Microsoft employees connected on a very high plane with IBM employees even with the 3200 miles that separated them. They were the only two companies that were privy to the project, while the rest of the world was kept in the dark about all aspects. For Microsoft employees however, the secrecy and security were a new piece of exciting intrigue that they had not encountered before; working in locked and reinforced rooms, covering the windows to the programming labs with paper to avoid unauthorized personnel looking in, using code names, locking documents in safes; it was all very exciting.

Finally, the project came to an end and outstandingly, Microsoft, a company that had a record of missing deadlines in many of their projects, was only a month late, after a few tweaks were made to the operating system at the request of IBM by none other than 86-QDOS architect Tim Paterson. The secrecy around the IBM PC had been maintained to the end. Only InfoWorld caught a whiff of the upcoming microcomputer by IBM and ran an article on it. Furious, Bill called the magazine's editors and reprimanded them for publishing rumors. He knew that IBM regarded confidentiality in very high regard and feared that a breach in the iron-clad silence around the personal computer might cause the company to pull the plug on the project. Instead, IBM misdirected the press by announcing a computer along the lines of their previous endeavors.

Bill, having previously bought all rights to 86-QDOS, was still in the clear. He had won the right to own the operating system despite facing off with Pertec again. The company was then offering Seattle Computers a hefty payday of

$250,000 to Microsoft's $50,000. The only reason Microsoft won the rights to 86-QDOS was Paul Allen's good relations with the Seattle Computers ownership; the fact Microsoft was the employer of 86-QDOS architect Tim Paterson who still maintained a cordial relationship with Seattle Computers; and the fact that Microsoft was offering technical support for the OS and good deals on their BASIC, as well as giving Seattle Computers a very favorable licensing deal to continue selling their computers with QDOS. Bill Gates bested his own lawyers by changing agreement documents and having them stipulate that Microsoft was buying, not licensing, the 86-QDOS. After Seattle Computers signed the contract, Microsoft, not them, owned the fastest OS in the world at the time.

Having delivered all aspects of the IBM deal, Bill was now secure in the knowledge that his company would soon be reaping the benefits of that partnership. But instead of sitting back and enjoying the fruits of his hard work, Bill Gates was already working on the next frontier of Microsoft expansion. He had held back from the operating systems business because he and Gary Kildall had agreed to keep off each other, but Gary had, even before the IBM deal came through, started bundling his CP/M operating system with a BASIC program from a Microsoft competitor. Bill obviously felt that by infringing on the computer language market, Gary was calling off their agreement. He would feel justified to explore the operating system market.

It was time for Bill to go head to head with DRI in the operating systems industry. The OS IBM had procured from Microsoft was named simply DOS, short for disk operating system. With full rights to market it at their discretion, Bill renamed it MS-DOS. When IBM released their new personal computer, Microsoft, as owner and not sub-licensees to the 86-QDOS, made good money on every sale. And when IBM compatible computers started shipping from 1982, Microsoft was there to provide both the BASIC languages and the operating system. Eventually, MS-DOS, not CP/M, became the industry standard in operating systems. Even though Gary received some reprieve when IBM reached a deal with his company Digital Research Institute, it came too late. He made another blunder and priced it way too high, practically handing the industry over to Bill Gates. Bill had decided to compete with Gary and won hands down.

Chapter 6: The Take-off of Microsoft

The year was 1981 and Microsoft was now making tens of millions in annual sales. His vision for the future of personal computers shifted to Graphic User Interface (GUI) after looking at the Macintosh in a confidential viewing. For two years, Apple engineers had been working on the Macintosh, with GUI being a key feature. While Apple had come out with graphic user interfaces first, they did not invent it. Steve Jobs had gotten the concept from Xerox.

Bill Gates knew that GUI would be huge but he didn't have a concrete idea yet how it could be incorporated into the Microsoft product range. In 1982, the GUI project started to explore practical applications for GUI. One idea was to create an interface manager that would integrate MS-DOS and software applications, making it easier for users to tend commands and use the software. It would be called, quite literally, Interface Manager.

GUI was due for an explosion in the early '80s. At the same time when Microsoft was working on Interface Manager, VisiCorp announced that it was working on what they were calling VisiOn, a GUI program that would go into the IBM PC and perform similar functions to Interface Manager.

In the meantime, Apple finished working on and released the Macintosh featuring the first ever mouse. The Macintosh was an instant hit, even though it was extremely pricey. The age of GUI had just been ushered, but Microsoft was not even near coming out with a new product to capitalize on the opportunity.

Bill and everyone at Microsoft knew that their GUI project was still in its infantile stages, but no one else needed to know that. In fact, why not tell everyone that we are in the advanced stages of developing an interface manager? While we are at it, let's tell them that ours will ship before VisiOn does. So that's what Bill Gates did in January 1983, the world would wait two years to see the first version of Interface Manager- but I am getting ahead of the story.

In the year 1981, Bill Gates was the majority shareholder and president of the company and he was growing ever more influential. Apple computers had made their initial public offering the year before and made its founders' instant millionaires. Bill had always known that

Microsoft would ultimately go public, but he did not want to hasten it. Even though Bill never attended any business school, he had a sharp business sense that had been honed further during his time lazing around at Harvard College. While other students read recreational magazines, Bill had preferred industry journals and magazines, teaching himself the art of business management. It is in part because of his business acumen and the study of business texts that he had managed to hold down the fort even in the earlier days when there were no qualified business managers.

He also enjoyed the support of loyal top management, including Steve Ballmer; a Stanford educated business manager who still deferred to Bill Gates' leadership in Microsoft business affairs. The two would start a Microsoft practice late in 1981; a company-wide meeting of boisterous employees, bringing them to a frenzy as they gave impassioned speeches on the future of the company. The company's sales and profits would be announced during this meeting, and the excitement of having surpassed the previous year's record would be a source of great rejoicing. The passion of Bill Gates when it came to Microsoft knew no bounds. It has always been the thing that has brought out the fierce competitor in him and inspired him to go out of his way. The attempts to outdo last year's meeting with funfair would culminate with him riding into the gathering with a gang of Harley Davidson motorcycle riding bikers.

As the company took off with consistently higher sales every year, the number of employees exploded in direct proportion. The IBM project, in particular, led to an explosion of employees that necessitated the relocation of Microsoft's corporate headquarters to a different location. The Northup Building off Interstate 520 was chosen as the ideal location; accessible, spacious, and conducive to the college fraternity-like environment of Microsoft.

Another major change that occurred at Microsoft in the year 1981 was a restructuring that turned the partnership between Paul and Bill into a corporation in which the two owned shares. Stock options would be easier to grant to employees with a more structured business structure. And stock options were important to employees, especially the senior managers. Steve Wood, the predecessor to Steve Ballmer as the second-in-command to Bill Gates, had left the company in part because the work culture did not favor him, and partly because the company did not have stock options at the time. A board was appointed, with Bill Gates being elected as its chair and Chief Executive Officer, and Paul becoming a company director. With an eye to the future, Bill brought into the Microsoft shareowners fold a venture capital firm named Technology Venture Investors with a sale of 5% of Microsoft for one million dollars. With one of the company's managers sitting at the Microsoft board, Bill had just ensured that he would receive expert consultation with the company when the time came to take the company public.

Another thing would happen in late 1981 that manifested some of the personality traits that the whole world would soon associate with see Bill Gates. As he started the long term plans to diversify the product range of Microsoft's computer languages to COBOL and FORTRAN, he came up with another top priority; knocking Digital Research Institute off the market and taking it out of business. Operating systems would now be the core focus of Microsoft, and the president wanted each and every one of his employees to pitch in. This idea of knocking the competition clear off the field instead of just creating products that sold better than the competition would shape Microsoft business practices for decades and culminate in the antitrust trial of the late 1990s. In Bill Gates reasoning, he concluded that there are benefits to reducing the number of competitors early on because there are fewer people to beat. In the case of DRI and their CP/M operating system, the competition wasn't all that huge. The company, late in releasing a 16-bit version of their legendary OS, still marked the price at a prohibitive cost which was four times that of DOS.

Still, Bill wanted the annoyance of having a strong competitor like DRI gone. One of the ideas he considered to accomplish this objective was giving away his DOS free to the public, flooding the market with so much software that CP/M simply did not stand a chance. The company could always make money on newer versions and technical support. That was the seriousness of Bill's determination to take down DRI; he was willing to hurt his own company if the objective was reached. In the end, he settled for creating serious buzz for DOS; so much so that CP/M was relegated to the underdog. In just one year, the CP/M had fallen from being an industry standard to an also-run. That is how serious Bill Gates was as a business rival. He capitalized on his own innovativeness to ensure that he pioneered new products, and he took every opportunity that had presented itself to propel himself forward, leaving competitors far behind.

The legendary negotiating tactics of wheedling and arguing with potential clients until they did things his way had now given way to some strong-arm tactics as the company's leverage grew. To convince manufacturers to buy a language program and operating system from Microsoft, he would withhold or dangle a different product and force the client to give him what he wanted. For example, the Digital Equipment Corporation wanted to offer Microsoft Word from Microsoft's consumer applications department with its forthcoming Rainbow minicomputer. But the company only planned to have it run exclusively on CP/M. As the leader in the minicomputer market, DEC was obviously a lucrative customer. Bill Gates insisted that if the company wanted to have his Word application, they would have to offer their clients the option of running the MS-DOS on the Rainbow. Even though Microsoft had no operational Word program at the time, the fact that it was under development was enough leverage for Bill to get a major computer manufacturer to fall in line and help him expand the reach of DOS. As a result, DRI would miss out on half the pie from what had been initially a slam-dunk opportunity to establish their operating system as a viable competitor to Microsoft. The gradual edging-out of a fierce rival was well on course.

In the end, the ease with which Microsoft frog leaped over DRI as the biggest operating system provider is unbelievable. So fast was the software industry in those days that DRI's six month delay in producing an operating system for the IBM PC, and the massive popularity of the IBM PC and its clones, scuttled all the chances that their CP/M operations system had of becoming an industry standard to the winds. This was always the modus operandi of Bill Gates in competition. While playing games as a child, he either won a game, or he practiced and spent as many hours playing the game as was needed to ensure that he came out on top. When he found out that he was not the best in mathematics back in Harvard, Bill decided to drop the subject as a career. When it came to business, Bill was either the industry standard or he was tussling with the industry standard for the title. With Gary and DRI, the fight for the top spot was relatively easy. It would not always be that way in his illustrious entrepreneurship career.

In this pursuit of utter annihilation of business rivals, Bill formed a marauding pack with Steve

Ballmer and the zealous Kay Nishi, Microsoft's agent to the Far East. These were the people who shared Bill's vision of domination and his predatory competitive style. Paul Allen was slowly being edged out of the picture as Bill Gates perhaps sought the company of more business-minded companions. The enthusiastic programmer with a keen business sense was quickly becoming the razor-sharp business executive with a background in programming. The little programming that Bill did around this period was simply going over the code written by his employees, but by and large, he focused his energies on the corporate side of building a business empire. In an industry that was breaking new ground every day, Bill's vision and innovativeness was a priceless personal asset. It was no wonder that Microsoft adopted the motto; "We Set the Standard." It was very much inspired by the company's charismatic leader.

Strategic partnerships, like the one with IBM, were quickly establishing his dominance in the industry. The IBM PC sold spectacularly, increasing the number of personal computers that operated on the MS-DOS a few times over. With a large market developing, Bill continued to market the OS aggressively. Even with a comfortable lead over CP/M, Bill never rested. Despite his fiercely competitive nature in taking out rivals, he was also great at competing with himself and taking his initiatives to the greatest heights possible. An upgrade to MS-DOS, DOS 1.1, was ordered in 1981 and completed in 1982. In the same year, Bill got his team to start working on a DOS 2.0 for IBM's next generation PC to follow in the success of the first one.

For a long time now, Microsoft had been a predominantly Business-to-Business software manufacturer, doing little business with the end user. So far, the most lucrative deals the company had made were all in the licensing of the BASIC programs and MS-DOS operating system. B2B operations were pretty straightforward because all the company had to do was study the industry and figure out where the next big thing was likely to come from and position the company accordingly. With the IBM PC targeted at the business community, a very real utility for computers was born. Bill Gates had earlier envisioned a computer in every home, much like the television. This vision of creating a personal computer that could be used by every person would be brought to life by Kay Nishi in 1982 with the first laptop computer. The portable computer was luggable and small by the standards of the times, but bulky by today's standards. It would be a few years yet before the personal laptop computer caught on.

What was gaining in popularity at the time was a real "a computer on every desk" situation, except that the desk was turning out to be the work desk, not the entertainment desk at home. After a humble start as a hobbyist kit back in 1975, the personal computer was fast replacing the ledger in offices in record-keeping among other tasks. Application software was the future of the software industry, and Bill Gates was being left behind. It is not that he did not know that application software was the future-- he had made the realization at the 1979 National Computer Conference-- he had just gotten distracted with the IBM project. He would have to play catch with MicroPro, the company that had prompted him to start the consumer products division of Microsoft, and VisiCorp, another applications software manufacturer that had written the VisiCalc software and was dominating the apps industry.

Bill Gates may have entered the applications software market late, but he intended to win. He would challenge the dominance of VisiCorp in the spreadsheets market with Microsoft's own software initially named Multiplan. Unable to supervise the project himself, Bill had appointed a Hungarian programmer by the name of Charles Simonyi who had made his start in professional code-writing as an employee of the Xerox Palo Alto Research Center (PARC). It is from Xerox PARC that Charles became acquainted with the Graphical User Interface, a nifty little innovation that would very soon take the whole computer industry by storm.

Bill Gates has been accused on numerous occasion of plagiarizing the products of rivals, sometimes leading to suits. His policy on creating products seems to have followed a very suspect method in the 80s. He simply analyzed a competing product and came up with ways to improve on their designs: not exactly blatantly stealing his competitors' products, but definitely getting inspiration from them. It would lead to a suit from Apple later in 1988, which Microsoft won, but it still underlined the claims of copying. The tactics definitely fall on a grey area. In one hand, neither Bill Gates nor Microsoft ever copied from their rivals. On the other hand, Bill did hire a consultant to study VisiCorp's spreadsheet program and suggest ways through which the software might be improved, both functionally and aesthetically. The Multiplan was hailed as a great product, but it could not hold a candle to the VisiCalc in terms of sales. It was a good entry into the software applications market, but the domineering Windows suite of software applications was still some years away.

In the meantime, the restless and ever-active Microsoft President/Chairman/CEO was eyeing new markets and started an International Business Division of the company to spearhead the entry into Europe, which Bill believed to be the new growth region for the computer industry. He wrote his first business plan for the International Division, having built a multi-million dollar business without drafting a single one. While the entry into the European market may be seen as the next obvious avenue for Microsoft's growth, it happened to the only place Digital Research was doing really well, having entered the market a few years before. It was the one region that could be a stronghold for DRI to compete with Microsoft, but with subsidiaries in a handful of capital cities in major European countries, Microsoft was soon giving DRI sleepless nights in the market too, and as MS-DOS personal computers started flooding into these markets, edging them slowly out.

Microsoft was facing the same problems companies that are experiencing rapid growth face, namely stretching their human resources too thin. Money was never a problem for the company, because Bill was a thrifty spender. He held the same beliefs about spending the company money as he did with handling his own; it was better off accumulating in the bank. It was a great security to have operations covered for a full year but still making more money. Rather than buy fancy stuff and have a good old extravagant time, he flew economy in all his flights, forced all his employees (even the senior management staff) to do the same, and frowned on Kay Nishi when he charged the company precious dollars by flying first class every few weeks, living in fancy hotels, and dining in the best restaurants. If Bill had anything to say about it, any travelling party he was part of did the exact opposite.

Bill held a rather romantic view of the small company with a few hundred employees. He wanted to maintain the small number, but during the 1980 IBM project, the company hired actively. Steve Ballmer would soon have his hands full recruiting employees to take up management positions as Microsoft started expanding, exploiting new markets, and releasing new products with increasing frequency. Old managers, good personal friends of Bill who had been with him from the beginning, left the company and were replaced by more experienced executives who had the requisite skills and experience to take the company to the next level. One such old executive was Vern Raburn, the man Bill Gates had placed in charge of the Consumer Products Division. As the company grew and Bill decided that application software would be the future of Microsoft, he sought to bring in an executive who possessed the qualities needed to head the division. Even though Vern was a great personal friend of Bill's (Bill would later be the best man at Vern's wedding), he asked him to resign or face the sack. The idealistic views of a small company with just a handful of employees would not blind Bill to the needs of the company. As usual, he proved very capable-minded when making business decisions.

Bill Gates' views that the application software industry was the growth sector of the future were further reinforced by an article on the Time Magazine in January 1983 that decried the shortage and poor quality of application software in the market. There obviously a huge market for good software, and Bill was of the opinion that other software companies were producing substandard applications, views that had been expressed in a Money magazine article the year before. It also echoed the 1976 open letter to hobbyists that introduced the world to

Bill Gates' ideas concerning software; his belief that great software was indispensable for the computer industry to flourish was deep-founded. However, in his first attempt after the Money magazine feature in November 1982, Bill failed to produce a great product. The Multiplan application was one-upped by a new entrant into the spreadsheet applications market, Lotus Corporation's Lotus 1-2-3. It was ten times as fast as Multiplan, and the consumers rewarded Lotus Corporation by making it the industry standard.

It was a huge loss for the man who was accustomed to winning all his life, but as he had proved before and would continue to prove over time, Bill Gates was a very good student of experience. The lesson Bill learned in this defeat was very important. It was also particularly humiliating because the Lotus 1-2-3 ran only on his MS-DOS, which meant that he was being beaten at his own backyard. His product had failed because it had been designed for too many platforms, sacrificing quality for versatility in some way because there was still no standard in operating systems that could allow a product to reach a big enough portion of the market. CP/M was still competing with MS-DOS for the sole position in operating systems, and there were a few dozen other platforms. It is safe to say that the realization that Multiplan failed because it had to be customized to dozens of operating systems added fuel to Bill Gates' conviction that a single dominant OS was better than many competing ones. He would be the one to create such an operating system. Then he could come up with superior application software to run on this operating system.

In the meantime, he introduced a few of the competitions practices that would get him rebuked a decade later. The Lotus ran solely on the MS-DOS, which Microsoft controlled. When he created DOS 2.0, an upgrade on the DOS 1.1 produced for the IBM Extended Technology (XT) personal computer, Bill Gates led a group of programmers in covertly inserting bugs that caused the Lotus spreadsheet to crash when loaded. It was the only time that Multiplan performed better than the Lotus 1-2-3 in the retail market. The introduction of bugs to his own product that enabled him to take down, even for just a short time, a rival, was the first taste of Bill leveraging one division of Microsoft to bolster a different one. It would lead him down a path of ethical grey practices that would make his name infamous all over the software industry.

Chapter 7: Growing Pains

Paul Allen's role in Microsoft had always been an important one. And while Bill did not include him in the inner circle including Kay and Steve that plotted the crushing of rivals, Paul was, like Bill, becoming more of a business leader than a programmer. They were not as close as they used to be though; the time and the strain of running a fast-growing business had driven a wedge between them. It is not that anything happened to rock the strong friendship of a few years ago, but the two just drifted apart. Paul Allen was a married man who socialized freely with employees at Microsoft, and Bill was a bachelor whose whole life entailed Microsoft and was considered aloof and rather arrogant by many people who came in contact with him. At a time when Bill was demanding more and more from his employees, Paul desired a better work-life balance and took time off to play his guitar with his after work rock 'n' roll band and treat himself to a science fiction novel. All in all, Bill and Paul were no longer the best friends they had been. Nothing but life had happened to force them apart.

Then in late 1982, the relationship between the co-founders was thrown into even greater turbulence by Paul's illness. He first felt it on a business trip to Paris; a feverish attack that had him excusing himself from a meeting to retire to his room. When the fever failed to ease after a day or two, he decided to come back home and seek medical advice from his doctor. He was diagnosed with Hodgkin's disease and advised to start chemotherapy right away. Remarkably, Paul continued working even as his hair started falling out due to the chemotherapy treatments, but only for a little while. The diagnosis and treatment regimen had changed his outlook on life. Accumulating great wealth and not really enjoying life was no longer an option for a man who had faced death so recently. He decided to leave Microsoft in 1983 to travel and spend quality time with his family. After years of spending 80 hours at the office and hardly ever taking a break, it was a welcome opportunity to rewind and appreciate the beauty of life.

The two co-founders would now see each other only during special days like birthdays, weddings, and Comdex. There are good chances that their relationship would have soured had they remained together. Tension was already developing between them. Bill thought Paul could work harder and goof off with his band less, and Paul hated having Bill Gates look through and sometimes change parts of his code like every other Microsoft programmer. After all, he was a shareholder. Paul moving when he did probably saved the relationship. The two continued being buddies and they would end up buying identical Porsche 959s in 1986. Unfortunately, they never got to race them. The cars did not meet US safety and pollution standards.

After leaving Microsoft, Paul had traveled around with his family for a while. His cancer had gone into remission, which meant that he could have a life again. His shareholding at Microsoft would do him a bunch of good once Microsoft went public as he, along with Bill, became an instant multi-millionaire. Despite attempts to bring him back on board, Paul decided to start his own software company named Asymetrix. His focus was on creating customizable software for Windows. His first product was announced the same weekend Bill announced Windows 3.0 in 1990, in the same city of New York.

And when every shareholder at Microsoft was celebrating the surge experienced by the Microsoft stock after the success of Windows 3.0, Paul Allen was right there celebrating the millions in money that came pouring into his bank account. However, unlike Bill, Paul Allen went on a spending spree, buying the Portland Trail Blazers in 1988 and getting them their own team airplane. He also bought himself a luxuriously fitted private jet that he flew to Portland every other weekend to watch his team play.

Bill Gates continued on at Microsoft without a hiccup. Paul had not been a confidante for a long time now, the position having been taken up by Steve Ballmer. The two had been communicating via e-mail for the last few months of Paul's time at Microsoft and rarely visited each other's offices. It was a friendship in decline, and there was hardly any remorse from either one of them. Granted, they were still good friends despite Paul leaving, but it was a less traumatic incident for Bill than it would have been in, say, 1979 before Microsoft experienced its growth spurt and became his whole life. Bill Gates took over the job responsibilities handled by Paul before leaving. He was now in a position to consolidate all day-to-day operations of the programming team under his keen eye.

In the meantime, Bill remained fixated on the future of the company. There were great new inventions in application software and Bill was right at the front, leading the pack. This new innovation was known as the Graphical User Interface (GUI). For any computer user today, it is hard to imagine using any computer without the point-and-click feature of the mouse, the touchpad, or the touch screen feature. But in the early days of the personal computer, only the keyboard was used to manipulate the computer. The story of the GUI is quite a glorious one, and because it would later become a point of lawsuits, it would be prudent to go into it.

The GUI was born in the Xerox PARC research complex, a facility out in Palo Alto that had come up with some of the more revolutionary technologies, including the Star computer. It was also from Xerox PARC that Steve Jobs had been inspired to create the Macintosh and Bill Gates got the idea to come up with the Windows operating system that made Microsoft a behemoth. Xerox PARC was handled as a separate entity from Xerox itself, meaning that the process of getting innovations from the PARC and getting them adopted into products for Xerox was long and often futile. The company bankrolled the operations, but they did not seen to have a definite plan to commercialize innovations from the Xerox PARC complex. The laxity at the company made the complex a fertile ground for tech companies to poach employees who preferred to stay at the forefront of the tech industry, coming up with real products rather than working for the sake of it. Charles Simonyi left Xerox PARC for this exact reason, preferring instead to join a company where his work would actually receive some utility in the market. And while these employees could not take products like GUI, they still had the knowledge of its existence and superiority. They also have a better idea of the programs that allowed graphical displays to work on a computer. Their bosses, illustrious and ambitious men as they were, would not be expected to let this knowledge go to waste.

The first Microsoft product to have the GUI was the Microsoft Word application developed with a view to take on MicroPro, the other applications software manufacturer that the company was facing off against. And just as with DRI in 1980, Bill's objective was to take the company completely off the market. But more importantly, every product developed at Microsoft from then on would use the GUI. Bill Gates guessed, correctly, that the graphical user interface would soon be the future of computing.

Just like the Multiplan application before it, Microsoft Word was far too sluggish to compete with the industry standard – WordStar. The naming strategy was decided upon after the senior management staff had bounced around a Multiplan product line, with Word being named Multiplan Word. But that would have meant sacrificing the association of the product with Microsoft. Furthermore, the company would have to run promotions for Multiplan as a separate entity if it had its own product line. There were more publicity benefits to be reaped by discontinuing the Multiplan name and simply naming all products Microsoft. Ergo, Microsoft Word.

The strategy was the brainchild of newly hired vice president of corporate communications, Roland Hanson. Roland represented a new breed of outsiders hired to take up management positions at Microsoft. It was no longer reasonable to hire from within for senior positions anymore; the company required more superior management skills and technical experience during this growth period.

Another recruitment made during this period was bringing in James Towne as company president. It went terribly because James was too business-oriented and tended to neglect the technical side of Microsoft, or didn't care to understand it. Even though Bill was increasingly losing his edge as a programmer as he worked exclusively in management, he was still very well rooted in the technical side of the business. He could use the lingo just as well as any programmer. It was one of those things that appear to be trivial but that meant so much.

Bill Gates wanted a manager with whom he could have a discussion on the technicalities of computer language. He could not respect James, a man who knew absolutely nothing about programming. Even worse, James did not care about learning programming technicalities. He felt strongly that Microsoft needed to adopt traditional management at this growth stage. Bill felt just as strongly that technically able managers were better suited to managing the highly technical Microsoft staff. The difference in opinions amounted to irreconcilable differences, and James reign as Microsoft president ended after eleven months.

Upon trying Microsoft Word out, Bill Gates sent an email to its chief programmer Richard Brodie pointing out the things he had disliked about it. It was a habit of his copied from John Norton back at TRW, but Microsoft employees had pretty much ignored the rants. Richard worked to make the changes suggested by his boss. It was a pleasant surprise for Bill to find out that his critique had been taken into account in subsequent prototypes.

Bill decided to flex Microsoft's muscle in launching the Word application. The total marketing budget was $3.5 million splurged on magazines promotions, free samples, and a feature in the Comdex show. The aggressive marketing strategy was successful, but only to a point. Reviews for Microsoft Word were mixed and users complained of difficulties in trying to use it. It required too much technical know-how. Rather than become a source of interest, the mouse intimidated users and affected sales too. A pattern was developing at the Consumer Products Division at Microsoft; the first version of application software was always a disappointment, but later versions would produce outstanding products.

And when the pressure of his job threatened to overwhelm him, Bill would take to the road to let off some steam. From a young age, Bill had always been a bit of a habitual traffic violator. After being arrested for speeding in New Mexico in 1977, he took his speeding habits to Seattle. He had always loved speeding, and he drove fast cars: the one indulgence he allowed himself in the midst of the frugality of economy flights and cheap hotels as the CEO of a highflying tech company. He even had a radar system installed in his car to enable him to evade police checkpoints, but the Seattle Police Department had introduced a helicopter to nab reckless speeding drivers. Bill's speeding record was so bad that he was at risk of losing his license. He decided to lose the Porsche 930 that allowed him to zoom around the freeways at 150 miles per hour for a slower Mercedes sedan. He pushed it to its limits too and totaled it spectacularly during his high school reunion.

Highway racing was the only outlet for steam accumulated after all-nighters at the office, staying as late as 2:00 am. He claimed to work better in these wee hours when the office was empty and the streets were quiet. Ballmer was usually Bill Gates' sidekick in these early morning working sessions, and the two would make decisions that the rest of the 9-5 managers would be expected to enforce. One of the reasons why James Towne left was because Bill did not consult (or inform) him on some very important decisions, and he would only learn later that some critical strategic decision had been made without his input. Steve Ballmer was still the de-facto second-in-command to Bill even when the company had already hired one.

Perhaps the responsibilities of company

president, CEO, and chairman of the board were getting to be too much for Bill Gates. He started hunting for a replacement for Towne immediately after firing him. This time, rapport was as important as the skill-set the president would bring to the company. Bill's influence around the company was too great to accommodate a president with whom he was not in the best of terms. James Towne was a terrible mistake, but if there is one thing that Bill Gates can be credited for without doubt, it is the fact that he is a great student of experience. He has always possessed the ability to recognize his slip-up and fix problems to ensure that they don't haunt him in the future. In removing himself from the presidency and seeking to install someone with real experience in business management, Bill demonstrated a brand of humility that was rather uncharacteristic of him. But it was important to hire a president, and Bill Gates would not rest until he had found the perfect man for the job.

In August 1983, two months after Towne had left Microsoft, the president's office had a new occupant- John Shirley. John was already well acquainted with Bill and his ways, and he acknowledged that his prospective boss could be "difficult to work with." Perhaps it is this awareness that got him the job. After all, the fact that he knew his future boss might be a difficult co-worker and still applied for the position said quite a lot about his interest in working at Microsoft. But John had a huge advantage over business educated managers like Towne; he had come up through the ranks in a technology company (Tandy Corporation) culminating is a position as vice president of computer merchandising. Bill Gates trusted Shirley, having worked with him on a few projects over the years and negotiated dozens of deals with him.

His style of management was calming in a very turbulent environment. Bill and Ballmer were passionate, rather aggressive managers, with Bill particularly given to emotional outbursts, even during negotiations. Shirley was a logical thinker and a diplomat, balancing out some of Bill's confrontational tendencies. Within months of taking the position at Microsoft, he had led reforms that made the company more efficient, better at marketing, and improved on all the organizational weak spots. To avoid the confusion that had ruined Towne's stay at Microsoft, he made Steve the vice president of marketing, creating a more streamlined hierarchy.

With Shirley at the helm, Bill Gates dedicated

his efforts to the future of the company, a job he loved and in which he excelled. He decided to become the product strategist for Microsoft, in charge of coming up with products that would enable the company to take Lotus, their chief competitor at the time, down. It was a responsibility he took very seriously, and he started a tradition in which he would take a week off every year to think and strategize. That first year, he decided that Excel, codenamed Odyssey during development, would be the perfect product to take down Lotus. It was a giant leap forward from Multiplan. Excel targeted the same market that Lotus 1-2-3 had monopolized, Macintosh.

In 1984, Bill was working on Excel and Windows, which were both very labor intensive. Windows was the future of Microsoft, but Excel was the salvo that would help him bring Lotus down. Naturally, Bill decided to push Excel. He moved a few programmers from Windows to Excel to speed up its release. He was not discouraged by Apple's continued support for Lotus and their upcoming Jazz program. He did not even accommodate Steve Jobs when he suggested several changes to him that would have made Excel more like Jazz.

After a year of yelling and squabbling with

project managers, Excel was ready. As part of its development legacy, Excel would be the project that had sent a man to the ER; newly hired project manager Philip Florence whom Bill had forced to write code instead of just supervising. Perhaps overpowered by the immensity of his workload, Florence had suffered a heart attack shortly before Excel was released in 1984.

The application was faster and had more functionality, just the right combination to create a star product. If Bill could not take suggestions from Steve Jobs, he was very eager to have him at the launch. It was important that he love Excel, because the future of Microsoft depended on Apple licensing it.

Despite the high stakes riding on the success of the Excel launch, Bill Gates could not have been less concerned about grooming. He came to the venue rather disheveled, with his hair uncombed and clothes scruffy; he was too stressed about the presentation to care. The previous evening, the demo program had crashed the computer when Bill and his team had tried to run it in preparation for the big day. But the grooming was not new. Part of the job description of his secretary was to help make him presentable before important social engagements when he had neglected his appearance.

He need not have worried. Everyone present loved Excel, including Steve Jobs, who broke rank with Lotus and endorsed it instead. Bill Gates had used a little less than $1 million to launch excel to Lotus' $7.5 million promotion for Jazz, but Excel outsold Jazz a few times over. More importantly, Excel outperformed Lotus 1-2-3 on the Macintosh computer. Sales of the Apple computer that had experienced a slump picked up immediately. The place of Microsoft on the high table of computer software, which had been suffering serious damage with the continued delay of Windows, was re-established.

With Microsoft riding high on the success of Excel, Bill Gates agreed to a photo session with the Wall Street Journal for a national cross-promotional ad campaign. His grooming was too terrible for the photographer to take a decent photo: there were holes on his standard issue Microsoft branded sweater and a large patch of sweat under his armpits. The cameraman could not tell Chairman Bill that he could not take his picture because his sweater had holes in it, or because his shirt was dirty, so he kept making excuses while a manager at Microsoft worked behind the scenes to make his boss presentable and avoid embarrassment. Finally, an employee had to be called in to give him his shirt for the photo.

By the time the cameraman was half satisfied with his looks and was starting to click away, Bill had had enough. He ordered everyone out of his office. There was far too much work to do around the office for him to let a bunch of media people to waste his time with camera angles and lighting. The Wall Street Journal hair stylist would be forced to take an airbrush to Chairman Bill's photo to make his hair presentable. Bill never knew; neither would he have cared. His company was facing more serious challenges.

In 1984, Bill Gates was 29 years old. He had already appeared in the covers of Time, Money, People and a handful of other magazines as a computer whiz making waves in computer software. Some of the articles were disparaging, but some were flattery in their praise of his rare genius. His only other comparison in popularity as a computer whiz was Steve Jobs, the man who had given the world Apples I and II and the Mac. Jobs' expertise lay in marketing and not the technical side of computer manufacturing (that is where he had had his start anyway, marketing Steve Wozniak's Apple I), and Bill

Gates disdained him for it.

Many of his younger employees at Microsoft were already raising families at this time, but he remained too dedicated to the company. The portrayals in the media of an awkward, extraordinarily intelligence and highly competitive man were not entirely wrong. Bill Gates had grown under a set of circumstances that gave his life sort of a protected growth curve to it. For once, he had not known failure ever since starting the Lakewood Programmers Group, Traf-O-Data, and Micro-Soft. Apart from a few isolated instances, his success was not brought by luck either. He had worked hard all his life to create an empire that was still growing. It demanded all his time, energy, and mental capacity, and he willingly gave it all. In business, his independence and abilities could not be questioned. Social life was a different thing altogether.

The only information on Bill's dating life around this period came from a Time magazine feature in 1984. Her name was Jill Bennett and she worked for the Digital Equipment Corporation and the two had been dating for a year when the article appeared. Their mutual appreciation for computers had brought them together after meeting at a dinner party. She harangued Bill on Microsoft's failure to get into 32-bit technology, which prompted him to christen her 32-bit (arguably the most romantic name a man like Bill Gates could give a girlfriend). The relationship was plagued by time conflicts, or more accurately, Bill Gates' time conflicts. He was singularly dedicated to Microsoft, putting in as many as 17 hours a day, every day of the week.

In the article in which Jill was interviewed, she gave fresh insights into the man Bill was in 1984. Behind the tough world of business, he was sensitive, passionate, and quite the mama's boy. The sensitivity was hidden well to protect himself from being taken advantage of, she asserted. The family was supportive of Jill when they met her, and she liked them because they provided Bill with much-needed emotional support.

She was a smart, beautiful woman, but in the end, the two were forced to split up because Bill just couldn't take the time off from Microsoft to cultivate a romantic relationship. He just wasn't ready. They parted on good terms and decided to remain friends.

A few months later, he started going out with a business woman named Ann Winblad. She was older than Bill, but the two got along spectacularly. She found him to be an interesting, exciting man with an unquenchable thirst for life. When he was not being the mean boss of Silicon Valley, Bill was a sweet, if a little distracted, lover. Recalling the old days of the Mc-Govern-Eagleton buttons, Bill would once sublease their car to hippies on a vacation, forget to bring a change of clothes on another, and crash a hang-glider into bramble shrubbery.

According to Ann, Bill was also a great storyteller. He could dramatize scenes to get his story across, much to her amusement, and often that of other patrons in a hotel too. The two had great chemistry. By 1987, they had travelled the world together and enjoyed each other's company a lot. But Bill still was not ready for a commitment and Ann, now in her late-thirties, could not wait around anymore. The two broke up and Bill went right back into the dating field.

One of the women he approached was a red-haired Microsoft product manager named Melinda French who caught his attention at a company picnic later that year. He asked her to dinner in two weeks, but the recent Duke University graduate was not having any of that. She wanted more spontaneity if she were to go out with him. All the same, she gave him her number and asked him to give her a call when he was ready to take her out sooner than "in two weeks." Bill called that very evening and despite the challenges of having a workplace romance, the two decided to try it anyway. The on and off relationship was the best kept secret of Bill's life for close to a decade, in part because unlike his previous serious relationships, Melinda tended to be very private and averse to granting interviews to magazines.

Chapter 8: Windows

By this point, the GUI was improving the usability of computers and making them increasingly easier to use. But only application software was using GUI. Operating systems were still woefully hard to use, requiring the user to have some skills in programming. A vision was born in Bill's mind of the day when the IBM PC and compatible machines would run on user friendly programs that anyone could use.

Bill no longer wanted to be burdened by all the intricate day-to-day operations of Microsoft. That is why a president was so important to hire. A strategic product manager was better suited to his "pushing boundaries" personality. His first project as manager in charge of product strategy was Microsoft Windows; an ambitious OS that would make the personal computer so easy to use his mother would be able to use it. The research project started in 1981 would now be taken to the next level in one of the biggest programming undertakings of the company – an operating system built on the GUI exploratory project he had started in 1981, and it would test the limits of him and his company in a way that no other project had done before.

The interface manager was a new, ground-breaking product. It was the kind of innovation that got Bill excited. He had not had cause for this much excitement since the Altair had come out and he and Paul worked all hours to write that BASIC program. Now, with a lot more resources at hand, he could afford to fly in executives of computer and software companies to share his vision with them. A vision in which everyone was using his graphical interface and VisiCorp was a non-entity. His product portfolio was quite impressive and there were more in the pipeline. Most notably, Interface Manager, the software that would enable users to have more than one task running on their computers, organized in sections called windows. Just like in the old days, he had promised that the program would be done in just one year.

Before the world could see this amazing product, however, it would take a few years of development. In that time, there were numerous release push-backs and a name changes. Rather than Interface Manager, the program would be named Windows, borrowing on its functionality of subdividing tasks on the screen into windows. The recently departed corporate communications VC Rowland Hanson was responsible for the renaming idea back in 1983. Now every time someone mentioned the new method of "windowing" more than one program on a computer, they would indirectly reference Microsoft's product for that very task!

Bill was obsessed with Windows. He had always been. But in 1985, galvanized by the success of Excel, he went into high gear. He strove to push Windows to computer manufacturers like IBM and Compaq, among others. He faced resistance from an unexpected end, IBM. Even though the company had outsourced the operating system for their first personal computer to Microsoft, and even though the success of that partnership had given birth to other companies like Compaq whose claim to fame was making IBM-compatible PC's, the computer giant balked at the idea of again outsourcing their GUI application to Microsoft. Instead, IBM decided to design its own GUI named Topview. The GUI scene was fast becoming too crowded.

The skills of former Xerox employees, having pioneered the graphical user interface, were now in very high demand. Bill Gates had been relying on the skills of his Xerox alumni Charles Simonyi, but now he realized that he would have to reinforce his team. He brought on board Scott MacGregor, Dan Lipkie, and Leo Nikora. With these three men on board the Windows project, Bill anticipated better progress. But nine months after he had made the announcement that his Interface Manager would ship before VisiCorp's, the latter announced an impending product release. Quarterdeck, a new software company, announced a GUI called DESQ. Second behind VisiCorp may have been fine, but coming third behind a nonentity like Quarterdeck was totally unacceptable. Chairman Bill was livid.

In an attempt to stem the expected hemorrhaging of customers from Microsoft, he decided to announce his own user interface. This practice would be branded as 'vaporware' and the software companies actually seemed to compete in that too. It served the purpose of ensuring a company's customer base that their vendor was busy at work and would be releasing a product soon. The 'busy at work' part was always true, but the 'soon' part was always subjective.

As Bill Gates tried to salvage the GUI situation, rushing to New York to make an announcement for Windows before a prototype was even ready, the partnership with IBM was falling apart. Not only was IBM moving away from Microsoft for its GUI with its own proprietary Topview, the company had also taken a stand against

Windows by endorsing VisiOn. It would become a distributor. Not to be left behind, Bill had convinced pretty much every other computer EOM Company (apart from Apple) to jump on board the Windows bandwagon. Afraid that IBM would knock them off the market, 24 PC manufacturers rallied behind Windows; a credit to Bill Gates' powers of persuasion.

In the end, Bill did manage to get Microsoft ahead of VisiCorp and Quarterback in some ways: he was the first person to demonstrate the power of GUI to the press and public. So in a way, he inserted himself into the narrative on the GUI, even if his part of the story, at least until Windows came out in 1985, was that of an executive aggressively promoting his company's vaporware. After this bit of damage control, Bill and Scott MacGregor, who had accompanied him to New York for the fake announcement, dashed back to Seattle to continue working on the Windows.

Bill's old workaholic habits persisted. The office was his home, and he would be coming and going at all times of the day and night. Sometimes there would be just enough time to race home, take a one hour nap, shower, and run back to the office for a meeting. It was in some ways a source of pride for him to put in all these hours and continue functioning, although many people would argue he was not functioning very well. His personality around this time is a bit of a contradiction. He knew the extension number of every employee in the programming department, knew even the registration plate numbers on their cars. He was also given to temper tantrums, turning apoplectic when anyone angered him and ranting about all sorts of perceived slights. The genius intelligence came with a superiority complex to match it, and he used every opportunity to prove that he was more intelligent than everyone else. Former programmers have recounted that Bill was always trying to one-up them during technical staff meetings, insulting not just their efforts but their intellect too.

Another accusation thrust upon Bill was the fact that he was still, despite his achievements and brilliant intellect, very immature. By his own words, he felt that he needed to grow up even in his late twenties. In fact, James Towne tells a story that transpired before he had been fired. He had been traveling on business with Bill when, just as they were leaving the hotel lobby, Bill remembered that he had left his luggage in his hotel room. He asked Towne to fetch the carry-on, and he had to pick up Bill's underwear from the floor before bringing the luggage down.

And while the temper tantrums and the foul moods during the period when the Windows project was going through numerous delays can be excused as simply being an outlet for the pressure accumulated by these failures, Bill was also reacting to a situation that he had never faced so far in his life: resistance and hardship. From the Sermon on the Mount to BASIC and MS-DOS, everything had always lined up perfectly for him. The resistance and feelings of failure from Windows were all alien feelings to him. He did not have the maturity of Shirley to take everything in stride.

From the time Bill Gates established the GUI project and put a team on it, there was a sense that it would be a strategic product. There was no doubt that the graphic user interface would revolutionize the industry, and throughout its life-cycle, Bill insisted on doing everything right to ensure that his precious Windows would be flawless when it finally made it to the shelves. This pursuit of perfection actually delayed the project a whole lot. While the strategy of Microsoft in the past few years had always been to hit the market with a product- however bad- and then release upgrades later, Windows received a very rarefied treatment. Everything had to be right; every feature had to perform just perfectly. Perhaps Bill gates decided that since he could not make it first in the market, he would make up for the delay by releasing such a great GUI that it would knock every other competitor out of the market.

Whatever his reasoning, one thing is for sure. Programmers who worked in the project recounted instances where their boss changed the product specifications of the Windows midway through the project, forcing them to scrap everything they had done before and start anew. It did not happen once either, it was a constant barrage of new features and revised rules. Not even the Xerox team could be given a free hand on the project. Nikora, as marketing manager of the consumer products division, advised Bill to release the Windows as is and improve later. He countered by insisting that Windows had to be head and shoulders above other GUI products in the market. In the end, a product that had started as a simple GUI application had evolved to become a fully functioning operating system, the first OS to incorporate a graphic user interface.

But the longer he delayed, the longer the industry questioned his strategies, and the more the pressure he felt from his early announcement. VisiCorp had long released their VisiOn GUI, but Windows was still in product development. In Bill Gates' psyche, the year may as well have been 1975 as he languished in school, knowing that his future was out there, but fearing that the timing wasn't right, finding an excuse to delay taking the leap a day, a week, a month longer. So many were the delays that even software publishers did not create apps to run on the Windows GUI. As the leader in operating systems, the delay of Microsoft to release their graphical tool was actually hurting the industry. VisiOn by VisiCorp had made fewer sales than expected and the company was soon struggling to stay afloat. Quarterdeck was suffering a similar fate.

One of the victims claimed by Windows was the advertising maestro Rowland Hanson. Unable to take the pressure of working under the pugnacious and irritable Bill of 1983-1985, he had left the company late in 1984. While finding his replacement in February 1985, Bill decided to reorganize, spinning applications and operating systems into different standalone divisions. Steve Ballmer, with similar modus operandi in motivating employees to work harder, would take charge of operating systems and be in charge of ensuring that Windows would ship before the end of the year. Ida Cole, one of the first female executive at Microsoft, would lead the charge in the applications division. Jean Richardson became the second female Vice president, replacing Rowland at corporate communications.

The early 1985 reorganization was just one of the many contingency measures Bill Gates put in place while pushing Windows to the finishing market. The other actions were not so constructive, but they affected the company just as much. As the release date neared, he became even more demanding and clashed constantly with programmers and executives alike. Nothing anyone ever did was enough. The nerves were killing him.

His newly hired VP of applications Ida Cole suffered the brunt of his frustration one September afternoon when she met with Bill to discuss some human resource challenges in her division. Philip Florence, the project manager who had suffered a heart attack the year before in the run-up to its release, had recently returned to work after a few months off recovering. Bill was concerned that he was not performing and wanted Cole to fire him. Hurting from a recent surgery herself, Ida refused to do that and Bill was incensed.

She decided that she could not put up with the constant yelling and criticism. She talked with Shirley, who transferred her to the International division, leaving Chairman Bill to take up the vice presidency at applications to add to his overflowing to-do tray.

Programmers who worked with Bill on Windows questioned his abilities to deliver on a product as big as what Windows had grown to be in 1984. Apart from the goal changing, Bill engaged in other self-sabotaging actions like underestimating the time needed to deliver on a component of the project. The result was programmers constantly being pressured to work at impossible speeds and frustration when deadlines were missed.

When Windows was finally released during the fall Comdex in November 1985, it was in an anticlimactic event. Windows had been in development for over four years and it had cost Microsoft two of its Xerox haul of employees. The year before, Nikora and MacGregor had left the company over irreconcilable differences with Steve Ballmer, just two of a whole bunch of people who had been rendered jobless by the Windows project. Bill Gates had never been as intense about a product as he had been about Windows, and neither had Ballmer. The programming team working on Windows had had to endure an unprecedented amount of yelling and screaming in the course of the project. It had been a whole year since his announcement of Windows to a packed auditorium at the New York City Helmsley Palace Hotel.

The public had been waiting two whole years for the groundbreaking Microsoft GUI and one year since Bill had promised to ship Windows before VisiCorp could ship VisiOn; they were not exactly thrilled. On the night of the official 'real' release of Windows, Bill Gates had to endure a thorough roast that included a Golden Vaporware Award from InfoWorld Magazine.

But even after the numerous delays and constant tinkering, Windows flopped. It was too bulky for the slow speeds and tiny memory of personal computers in 1985. However, its features sure were cutting edge, with highly advanced features that were granted to revolutionize the computer industry. In the end, it underperformed not because it was terribly developed, but because it was a few years ahead of its time. It would not be until Windows 3.0 in 1990 that Microsoft produced a Windows program that matched the capabilities of processing units in computers at the time- the first really trendsetting Windows application.

Undeterred by the criticism directed his way after the Windows gaffe, Bill Gates was flexing the Microsoft muscle a day after the Comdex convention in which he was roasted mercilessly in front of hundreds of people. Apple was already claiming that Microsoft had copied their Macintosh operating system, thus violating their copyrights, but Microsoft was unrepentant. Moreover, he was eager to peek under the hood on the Mac technology again, and Apple would have to give him the permission to do so.

The claims by Apple that Microsoft was ripping them off stemmed from a 1982 agreement in which Microsoft was to partner with Apple to produce application software for the Mac. Obviously, Apple had to give Microsoft prototypes of the Macintosh and software tools to do their work. This was around the time when Bill was pushing GUI and working overtime to bring a GUI application to the market. Apple had been working on graphical user interface since 1979, so their technology was far advanced than Microsoft's. A few ideas from Apple ended up in the Windows, which the whole world (including Apple) had just seen.

On November 22, Bill Gates and a team from Microsoft sat with John Sculley, Apple's recent replacement for Steve Jobs, and his Apple top brass. Sculley was outraged and threatening to sue, but Bill calmly explained that with his company tied up in court defending Windows, they would be forced to cease working on the Excel and Word applications that Apple was relying on to revive sales for the Macintosh that had been on a downward spiral. Apple could not risk antagonizing Microsoft. The company was already laying off workers, their financial situation was so dire. And just like that, Bill had shifted the power back to Microsoft. The agreement signed on that fall day recognized that Multiplan, Windows, Excel, and Word contained displays derived from Apple's own GUI programs, but it also allowed Microsoft to continue raiding Apple's secret cellar of innovative GUI ideas meant to go into the Macintosh for their own products. In return, Microsoft would upgrade and improve the bugs-filled Word to reach acceptable levels of performance.

Bill was not done. The copyright concessions were not quite enough. After learning that Apple was planning to start making a proprietary BASIC program named MacBASIC, Bill was livid. He embarked on a mission to win back the rights to supply Apple with BASIC, again using the Excel program as leverage. Not only did he succeed in forcing the company to quit working on a BASIC program, he also managed to get them to sign over the MacBASIC name and all code written for the project so far over to Microsoft. It was an unlikely victory; a total and complete annihilation of a friendly rival that left the engineers who had been working on MacBASIC humiliated. One developer, Donn Denman, was so heartbroken when Sculley informed him of the scuttling of his project. He felt so possessive of it he considered it his "baby" and he could not understand how Bill could dictate to his boss what Apple could or could not do. How did that happen?

Both concessions won by Bill represented a masterpiece in negotiation. Microsoft was receiving a windfall while giving nothing away. In the ten years he had been running Microsoft, he had fine-tuned the skill of recognizing the weakness in a rival, and he was never shy to exploit the weaknesses for his own good. And while Apple was one of Microsoft's most valued partners, Microsoft was a bigger priority, and not even common interests would prevent Bill from taking advantage of a situation to win. However, in just a few years, these practices would come back to haunt Bill and Microsoft.

Discontent towards the business practices of Microsoft was building with every negotiation Bill engaged in. His strategy was to hold a gun to his competitors and partners alike, stopping at nothing to ensure that he won. He was too competitive and perhaps winning was too important to him. But from the ashes of his bested rivals would soon be rising a storm unlike any that Bill Gates or Microsoft had faced before as people started feeling more and more that Microsoft needed to be tamed and its competitive ways curbed. In the far horizon, a storm was gathering. But in the meantime, Microsoft was ripe for an IPO.

Chapter 9: Microsoft's IPO

The personal computer and software industry was the growth industry of America in the early 1980s. In just three years starting in 1980, three major companies had very successful public offerings. Apple had led the way in 1980 and received a $1.8 billion valuation. Steve Jobs had become an overnight multi-millionaire with a fortune valued at over $250 million. Three years later, Lotus Corporation had gone public too, as had Ashton Tate. In the software industry, Lotus was the leader at this time, followed by Microsoft, then Ashton Tate. Their stocks had all been very well received. So how could the extremely competitive Bill let his fiercest competition beat him to the stock market?

Bill Gates had always been quite the controlling manager, supervising every process of code writing by Microsoft programmers and even changing some. He enjoyed having full and unchallenged control. A public offering meant answering to shareholders on every decision he made, thus diminishing his authority, hitherto unchallenged. Coming from full power to do as he pleased to building consensus was not something Bill cared much for. For one, he was terrible at building consensus. His best decisions were those made in the wee hours of the morning after a sixteen-hour day.

Over at Apple, his ally Steve Jobs was going through a hard time. After taking the company public those five years before, his new board had been giving him a hard time over product direction. The Apple co-founder was being forced to convince his board that he was good enough to continue running the company. It was not a situation he was very eager to put himself in. A few months later, Steve Jobs was driven out of his own company in a hostile takeover and a new age of the relationship between Microsoft and Apple was ushered in.

Bill Gates was exactly 30 when Microsoft started putting in place the mechanisms that would allow it to hold its initial public offering in 1985. The following year would be Microsoft's twelfth as a company and its fifth after incorporation. The number of employees had exploded to about 1,200 and the number was increasing every week. The company had had to scout for a new location for its exploding workforce and now finishing touches on the company's new Redmond office campus were at an advanced stage, with employees expected to move in the next year.

The Securities Exchange Act of 1934 stipulates that a company has to go public if more than 500 employees own shares. Share options had been used to entice employees to Microsoft since the company had been incorporated and if Bill Gates did not do it himself, his company would soon be forced by government legislation to file public financial reports anyway.

The board was eager to take the company public, but as the CEO, Chairman, and majority shareholder, his decision would be the final word that would send Microsoft hurtling towards the IPO or clinging on to its private status a while longer. The only thing that had been holding him back was Excel and Windows; he had wanted to get them out to the public before starting work on the IPO. Now that they were both out, there was nothing holding him back. The day after he turned thirty, Bill gave the go-ahead.

Despite his hesitancy in going public, Bill Gates had been laying the groundwork for the IPO for about four years. In the 1981 incorporation, Bill had sold 5% of the company to David Marquardt who now sat in the Microsoft board. With his experience as a venture capitalist, Bill had in David a free consultant all through the exercise. The year before, Microsoft had hired

Frank Gaudette as the company's Chief Financial Officer. Frank was a veteran of public offerings having managed the IPOs of three other software companies before Microsoft.

A public offering was an area Bill was hopelessly inept at and he could not summon the passion to learn how to do it apart from the bare basics. He considered the business of business to be very boring. His business duties at Microsoft were only made pleasant by the fact that he sold computer software, a product he cared for massively. The financial businesses like banks and underwriters had never quite appealed to Bill.

Lotus Corporation had gone public in 1983, and Mitch Kapor, the company's chairman, had had a terrible experience from his underwriters. So Bill Gates was prejudiced against bankers when he started the process of offering Microsoft to the public. From the start, his attitude towards the whole financial institutions was rather frosty. He seemed to be tolerating them only because he had to. A dinner to which he had been dragged by Jon Shirley with Goldman Sachs, who would end up underwriting the IPO, was awkward and strained. He approved of their table manners, but he kept them at arm's length.

Following the recommendation of David Marquardt, Microsoft was using the services of two underwriters. One of them would be the standard Wall Street financial services firm to push the stock to institutional investors while the other one handled the more technical aspects of the IPO. Goldman Sachs had been chosen to spearhead the IPO out of a pool of numerous interested firms. The second choice was much easier because the firm's executives had been courting Microsoft for a few years. Alex, Brown & Sons would be the second underwriter to Microsoft's IPO.

As the internal due diligence activities stretched on, Bill Gates decided that if he would have to suffer through the tedious process of going public, then at least he would try to get something out of it too. After a few months of correspondence, Bill had granted permission to a Fortune magazine reporter to shadow him during the IPO. The job shadowing was meant to give the journalist as much insight into Microsoft as possible, showing readers the complexities of running a software company in the hope that his story would inspire other entrepreneurs. Goldman Sachs and the Baltimore based firm of Alex, Brown & Sons, the two firms with the honor of taking Microsoft public, tried to talk Bill out of doing the Fortune feature but he would hear none of it. He could do whatever he wanted and the two had no business trying to interfere. Of course this little antic did little to improve Bill's opinion of bankers.

The company was doing great, or so said the prospectus that Microsoft VP of corporate affairs had written. The senior leadership (Bill) wasn't greedy and he had allocated himself a very modest salary. Despite the failure of Windows 1.0 in 1985, Microsoft was still a very strong company. Other products like the Excel and Word were doing great in the open market and in the OEM licensing department too. Bill Gates had ordered work to commence on a new version of Windows immediately following the poor reception of Windows 1.0 in 1985. Commentators predicted a lot of interest in the company, with the stock price expected to shoot right through the roof.

But Bill Gates was not a happy man. The IPO was keeping him from his work. After releasing the prospectus, he had received dozens of calls from friends, family, and acquaintances who were interested in buying Microsoft shares. They wanted him to double up as their agent and allow them to buy shares through him. He could not concentrate on his core business, developing and selling software, while the IPO took up all his time. He was also concerned that the fluctuation of prices in the securities exchange after the initial public offering would make employees lose focus of the important thing, work.

When every obligation for the IPO had been fulfilled, Bill was obligated to go on a world tour promoting the stock. He recited the company's performance dutifully but could not help projecting boredom despite massive excitement among the bankers and institutional bankers who were targeted in the promotional tour. In the end, he found a way to have fun by selling Microsoft's products along with the IPO.

Upon returning from the promotional tour where he had seen firsthand the anticipation investors had for his company's stock, Bill decided that his underwriters could offer him a better price than the $16 per share he had previously negotiated. With observers predicting a price of up to $25 per share on opening day, Bill Gates decided that he was not in the business of making institutional clients rich. He would need a better price than $16. After a short period of haggling, Goldman Sachs convinced both their institutional clients and Bill to set the price at $21.

The underwriters were entitled to a predetermined 6.5% management fee for every share offered, but Bill learned that Sun Microsystems had gotten a fairer deal of 6.13%. Now that was something at which to beat a competitor! Bill insisted that he should also get as low a fee, but Goldman Sachs and Alex, Brown & Sons were willing to go only as low as 6.3%. Chairman Bill was unwilling to compromise and, deciding to take a vacation, he left strict orders to Shirley and Frank Gaudette to ensure that the management fee did not go higher than 6.13%. Frank, taking point on the negotiations, had managed to bring the fee down to 6.2% one night and the underwriters were equally adamant that the fee could not go lower than that. With Bill Gates out of the picture and unreachable in his sailing boat, Shirley accepted on his behalf. He might get pissed when he came back, but the company had come too far along the long process to give up over a few pennies now.

The MSFT stock opened in the morning of March 1986 at $25.75 a share, peaking at $29.25 before coming back down. It was one of the most successful initial public offerings and even Paul Allen came out of his silence to express satisfaction over the opening. With a 28% stake in Microsoft, he had just become a very rich man. As for Chairman Bill, plowing through books off the coast of Australia in one of his favorite reading vacations, the IPO could not matter less. There were more important matters to take care of.

Kay Nishi, the flamboyant Japanese entrepreneur who was responsible for Microsoft's great performance in Asia, had recently gotten himself in Bill's crosshairs. In the last couple of months, the ever unpredictable and impulsive Kay had angered Bill by using Microsoft resources (which he had always been quite liberal about spending) to promote his own products. Bill, himself a frugal person, had always disapproved Kay's extravagance. Bill had reached new heights of angry when Kay had staged a demonstration of the capability of Microsoft's software with a giant dinosaur outside Tokyo train station. Bill did not mind the demonstration, but he could not stomach the costs Microsoft had incurred: $1 million. He reprimanded Kay in strongly worded telegrams since it was all he could do.

The only reason Bill had ever tolerated Kay's extravagance was because he brought in the most business of any international division. And as if failing to dedicate himself fully to Microsoft and wasting Bill's hard-earned money was not enough, Kay Nishi was talking up specially designed microchips that could replace operating systems in computers. He had recently opened his own computer company ASCII, and he was spending more of his time working in it than he was spending pushing Microsoft products. Operating systems being Microsoft's bread and butter, Bill Gates saw the proposition as a matter of Kay attempting to cut off the arm that fed him.

Following the Tokyo train station demonstration, Bill had offered Kay a permanent job at Redmond complete with a generous stock package in a bid to bring him under control. Kay Nishi was not the kind of man to be tied down in one place or subordinated to a boss. He was too much of a free soul, too much of 'his own man' to even consider the job offer. In a last-ditch effort to reconcile their differences, the two met in the Microsoft office park in Sydney and flew together to Tokyo.

For three days, the two alternated between calmly discussing their visions for computing, yelling at each other, and apologizing profusely. Kay Nishi was one of Microsoft's oldest employees and a close personal friend of Bill's. Bill was unwilling to break ranks with a man he felt was more like him that anyone else he had ever met, but in the end, their differences were irreconcilable. Bill Gates terminated Microsoft's oldest partnership in the last days of March and immediately started drawing up plans to open a subsidiary.

In May 1986, Microsoft Japan opened its doors for business. In characteristic Microsoft fashion, their hiring gave no special consideration to their decade-long partnership with Kay. They poached a bunch of ASCII executives to work at Microsoft, an action that prompted Kay to publicly trash Bill Gates. Bill was only too glad to return the favor, pointing out that he was worth millions of dollars while Kay was in debt. And he knew that because he had personally advanced Kay money on several occasions previously.

Back at Microsoft's Northup complex offices, Bill Gates continued to steer the company to exceptional growth well beyond his own projections. He had adopted a diversified product range policy for Microsoft and as product strategist and applications VP he was responsible for supervising the development of flagship products like Windows, Word, and Excel. With works complete on the 29 acres Redmond office park, the 1,200 employees were moved into four futuristically designed buildings in which every person had a window office.

The office park was a self-contained work environment complete with four 7-Eleven stores- one for each of the four buildings- sports fields, and an artificial lake. The atmosphere at Redmond was reminiscent of a college campus park, a design choice made to foster camaraderie among the young workforce. The attitude went as far as allowing employees to hang posters or relics or whatever they wanted to hang in there to create their ideal workspace. Pranks were the order of the day.

There was another reason for the relaxed and permissive work environment. With all the fun and the freedom employees had while in their offices, it almost felt like they were having fun, not working. A peaceful work environment created an outlet of stress so that the 14 and 15 hour days took less of a toll on employees.

One of the reasons Bill Gates had hesitated with the IPO was his fear that it would distract employees from their work. Being totally unconcerned with his stock market net worth (it is all just paper), Bill was worried when charts showing the current price of Microsoft stock started showing up in offices and employees with stock options wearing badges that read "Fuck You. I'm Fully Vested."

The only indulgence Bill allowed himself was a speedboat. He had always wanted to take his passion for speeding from land to water and a speedboat was just the thing to get him there. But after spending the whole day looking around during a boat show, he settled for a $12,000 ski boat. He was worth hundreds of millions of dollars at this time but Vern Raburn, an employee, and friend who had accompanied him to the boat show, reported that Bill tortured himself over the purchase "like he was spending fifty million bucks."

Before the year 1986 was over, Bill Gates had hit the billion-dollar net worth mark. At 31, he was the youngest person in the history of America to achieve that distinction.

Chapter 10: Suits

If Bill Gates didn't much like wearing them, he definitely faced many in the decade or so after Microsoft had gone public. In December 1986, he was dragged to the first lawsuit as a defendant by Seattle Computer Products the original creators of the DOS that had brought Microsoft massive success and allowed them to challenge Lotus Corporation's position as the leader in computer software. He and Microsoft would face a handful of suits before the century ended.

The 1986 trial had been filed by Rod Brock. Six years before, he had been approached by Microsoft for a licensing agreement to give them exclusive rights to 86-QDOS- the only OS that was based on the 8986 microchip when IBM came calling at Microsoft back in 1980. Microsoft had not disclosed that IBM was their client, but Seattle Computers had agreed to the ownership swap because they wouldn't have managed to provide technical support to customers anyway. Their programmer had recently moved to a rival company. While Microsoft walked away with full rights, Seattle Computers had gotten a perpetual license to use MS-DOS on their computers free of charge for all eternity.

The company had recently encountered tough times and was going out of business which involved selling everything. Its biggest asset was the perpetual MS-DOS license. Rod chose to inform Microsoft about his impending sale of the perpetual license. If they could buy him out, they'd get their perpetual license back. He anticipated as much as $20 million for the whole company, but Microsoft insisted that the license was nontransferable and they had no interest in buying him out.

Just a few months prior to the case, Bill had bought out a company started by Tim Patterson (the architect of 86-QDOS who had had worked in Seattle Computers and Microsoft as well as a bunch of other companies before forming his own and actually the programmer who had moved to a rival company and forced Seattle Computers to sell 86-QDOS) for $1 million to recover a perpetual license that had been given to him by Paul Allen for his work in MS-DOS as a Microsoft employee.

Obviously, Bill was not averse to buying out a company to recover royalty-free licenses, so why go to trial with Seattle Computers? He was opposed to buying Seattle Computers' perpetual license as a matter of principle. Throughout the three weeks of trial, Bill insisted that he had bought the DOS once and Rod had no right demanding that he pay for it again. Paul Allen was among the witnesses who were called in to shed more light on the matter. Even after their best efforts, the lawyers representing Microsoft in the trial were not optimistic of winning the case.

As the jury decision approached, the lawyers finally managed to get Bill Gates to acquiesce and allow them to try an out-of-court settlement. After a few hours of tough one sided negotiations in which Microsoft kept increasing the settlement figure by $100, 000 every hour, Rod Brock's $60 million suit was settled for $925,000 while the jury deliberated. If Rod had refused to settle, there were good chances that he would have won. His lawyer, taking a straw poll later, found that a 10-2 vote would likely have been the outcome.

Ann Ribald, talking about her relationship with Bill Gates, intimated that he likes to live on the edge. In this case, Bill had pushed his chances with the Seattle Computers DOS license to the very edge. Had Rod won the case, Microsoft would have lost millions of dollars to the computer manufacturer who would have bought the license. Tandy Corporation, the previous employer of then Microsoft President Jon Shirley had expressed interest in buying the perpetual license. A combination of his 'push the boundaries' tendencies, and of course, his penny-pinching nature (refusing to pay for the 86-QDOS twice), had prompted Bill to take his chances even when it was too risky.

But the most remarkable observation from the trial was Bill Gates' attitude towards his partners. Talking about the trial later, the lawyer representing Seattle Computers intimated that Rod was willing to settle for half a million dollars. We can only hypothesize about the reasons Bill decided not to settle for that amount, but he ultimately did pay $425,000 more than he would have paid had he taken a more indulgent route in dealing with Seattle Computer. Bill decided to play hardball and while we may not be sure what would have happened had he been more willing to settle before the trial, it is safe to assume that the settlement would have been significantly lower.

These hardball tactics would endear and estrange Bill to different people in almost equal measure. Partners who expected Chairman Bill to be sympathetic to their cause in their dealings with Microsoft were almost always disappointed when they encountered a boss who wouldn't care less about their plight. Investors who put money on the Microsoft stock could rest assured that their investment had found a great custodian in Bill Gates. The actions of Kelly Korr, the lawyer who had squared off against Microsoft on behalf of Seattle Computers, demonstrates this fact better than anything else. After the trial, he decided that investing in Microsoft stock made perfect business sense. In Bill Gates, Microsoft had a leader who was cold-blooded in his pursuit of market share and success for his company.

An initial class suit comprising of players in the computer industry who had been screwed over by Microsoft were the first attempts to start a class suit, but the endeavor did not gain steam and it was dropped. However, the resentment was there and in some quarters it was very profound.

As for Kelly Corr, his skirmishes with Bill Gates were not over. His firm was hired to represent a group of Taiwanese businessmen who had been arrested with counterfeit Microsoft software not long after the Seattle Computers suit. This time the trial was held in San Francisco, and Microsoft was looking to make an impression on counterfeiting by nailing the businessmen. However, a problem arose in the pre-trial proceedings. Despite many promises made, the businessmen were not paying Corr for his services. He made an application to stop trying the case but Microsoft blocked the application. It was sweet payback to have their former adversary losing money in a trial they would probably never win anyways. Chairman Bill was not involved in this particular charade, but as Chairman and CEO, nothing happened at Microsoft that he did not know of or approve.

Even as the company's legal department tussled with lawyers in trial courts all over the country, the programming departments were busy developing the next generation of Microsoft operating systems and software. One such program that was under development in 1986 was OS/2, the follow-up to MS-DOS made for IBM four years previously. IBM and Microsoft were counting on it becoming the OS of the 90s. What it would do instead was rock the super-partnership to the very core.

The OS/2 had started as a quest by IBM to replace the DOS with something better to bolster their slumping personal computer sales. With the huge success of his previous partnership with IBM fresh in this mind, Bill was only too willing to develop OS/2.

The first dispute arose in the selection of the microchip on which to base the operating system. The 8086 line of microprocessors had proved to be more successful than the 8088 it had replaced, so Intel Corporation had recently released the 80286 microchip, a more powerful version of the 8086 and previous chips but one that was still sluggish by 1986 standards. Every programmer, including Bill Gates, considered the 286 'brain dead.' A more powerful microchip 80386 was expected within the year and this was the one on which every futuristic software was to be based.

Microsoft wanted to wait for it instead of using the 286. More functionalities and products to run on computers were necessitating more space in chips and storage systems. As it were, the DOS 3.0 version was pushing the 286 chip to the limits. IBM could hear none of it. The last two computers they had released had performed very poorly in the market and they needed a winning product quickly.

With a long history of working together to produce standard-setting products, it should have been easy for Microsoft to convince IBM to wait for the 386 chip. But IBM was a behemoth of a company and the man who was given responsibility for the project was not the same one with whom Microsoft had been doing business since 1980. Don Estridge had recently passed away, giving way to Bill Lowe, a man of little technical competence but considerable corporate experience. He insisted on basing OS/2 on the 286 chip and abandoning GUI to speed up the development process. Exactly the opposite of what Microsoft had proposed. Bill Gates was furious. He ranted to his executives during a strategic retreat, branding IBM's product strategy "f*#ked up."

 IBM would soon come to the same conclusion when Compaq, a computer that had started out as an unrepentant IBM clone, released a computer based on the 386 chip; the Compaq Deskpro 386. And just like that, the student had become the teacher. Compaq became the trendsetter and established its position in the computer industry as one of the big dogs. The sales of Compaq Deskpro 386 were massive and they were eating into IBM's market every day. Apple had also released the Macintosh and, boosted by Microsoft products like Excel, it was doing well too. With the competition closing in, IBM decided that it was time to call in the cavalry.

When Bill Lowe summoned Bill Gates to a meeting in New York in the spring of 1986, Gates expected to be told off for pushing IBM too much on the 386 microchip, maybe even lose the account. The meeting was the only time when Chairman Bill was given a dose of his own medicine. Both parties were desperate, but it was Lowe who recognized Bill's anxiety and decided to take advantage. He negotiated a deal that only succeeded in sending Microsoft into a wild goose chase, producing OS/2 for the 286 and 386 chip, a Windows for OS/2 that would be renamed Presentation Manager, and GUI revisions and insertion in IBM mainframes.

With so much work to do to retain the IBM partnership, Bill was forced to choose between OS/2 and his Windows program and IBM's Presentation Manager. So eager was he to please IBM that he even considered terminating Windows altogether. Steve Ballmer, his sidekick and VP of operating systems, was all for killing Windows altogether to focus on Presentation Manager. In the end, they decided to transfer the resources for Windows 2.0 (under development) and focus the bulk of their efforts on Presentation Manager and OS/2.

However, some pundits suggested that Bill only agreed to produce Presentation Manager as an indirect way to get Windows endorsed by IBM. All the same, development continued on OS/2 and Presentation Manager all throughout 1986 and 1987. A presentation of OS/2 on IBM's new PC/AT (advanced technology personal computer) was given to about 90,000 people at the fall Comdex in 1987. The reception at the event was warm enough to prompt opposition from an unexpected angle.

Windows was a rip off of the Macintosh in many ways. Bill Gates had signed a document admitting as much in 1985, right about the same time when he had forced Apple to allow Microsoft to use its GUI technology on the Windows. Apple Computer might be okay with Bill Gates ripping off their operating system to sell in the open market, but they could not let their own technology be used by IBM, their fiercest rivals, to beat them in personal computer sales. They filed suit against Microsoft for copyright infringement in San Jose federal court in March 1988 with absolutely no warning. How much of a surprise was it? Well, Bill Gates learned from the media a day after meeting with John Sculley and not a single word of resentment had been uttered. Bill was convinced that Apple was simply launching a broadside at Microsoft in the media to create a public relations crisis. And it was working. The

Microsoft stock dropped significantly on the day Apple announced the suit. If Microsoft lost, all its GUI projects including Windows, Excel, Word, and the contractual OS/2 and Presentation Manager would be thwarted.

Microsoft counter-sued immediately, arguing that Windows 1.0 had been licensed, thus all other subsequent versions would be protected from infringement claims. Besides, Apple had gotten the GUI technology the same way Microsoft came by most of theirs, from Xerox PARC. Although the suit had the immediate effect of putting a freeze on Microsoft's stock, there was no immediate injunction stopping the targeted products from shipping. OS/2 had started shipping in early 1988, but it did not need a court injunction to thwart its performance in the market. Industry observers predicted a flop based on the OS/2's exorbitant pricing and lack of compatible applications.

At 20 million registered users, DOS was by far the most popular operating system in America in 1988. Neither the users nor the software companies were willing to shift their operations from DOS to an entirely new operating system. In a glaring lack of insight into the product preferences of his own market, Bill publicly continued trying to push OS/2 to software companies, computer companies, and consumers alike. In a way, he was fighting against himself. However, behind closed doors, he was shifting resources away from OS/2 and turning back to Windows. Development works on the Windows 3.0 picked up steam in 1988. It was designed to operate on the more advanced 80386 chip and expectations of its performance were high. Windows 2.0 was doing considerably well.

More changes in management at IBM would further strain the partnership with Microsoft. Following the dismal performance of OS/2, Bill Lowe had been summarily fired. His replacement was Jim Cannavino, a man who did not trust Bill Gates and who believed that the Microsoft Chairman had duped Bill Lowe and led him down the path to failure. The decision by Bill to count his losses on OS/2 and focus instead on Windows and DOS was seen by IBM as a betrayal of trust. In all due fairness, the poor performance of OS/2 is all due to the decision by Bill Lowe to insist on creating an operating system for the 286 and 386 chips rather than focusing on one of them. Working on the two versions had created double the work for Microsoft employees and ultimately led to the poor performance.

The relationship between Microsoft and IBM fell completely apart after the fall Comdex in 1989. During the exhibition, the Bill and Lowe presented a united front on OS/2, announcing that some features of Windows would be stripped down and added to the OS/2 to improve its performance. However, before the event was over, Cannavino gave a solo press conference in which he seemed to indicate that Windows was being scrapped to pave the way for OS/2. The press conference gave Microsoft's rivals, including Jim Manzi of Lotus Corporation, ammunition to criticize Microsoft in the media. Bill Gates was not amused. He transferred a horde of programmers from OS/2 to Windows and decided to focus on developing Microsoft's flagship products. He had finally decided to untangle himself from the restrictive partnership with IBM and he would stop at nothing to be free. It was a simple business decision to support a promising product at the cost of another; it was just tough luck that IBM, a former strategic partner, was the opportunity cost to the decision.

Bill often went into the grey area in his bid to find the next big product for Microsoft. In 1989, Microsoft had encountered a product named Quicken during a joint promotion with other software companies in retail stores that sold software. Quicken was a money management product developed by a Silicon Valley company called Intuit founded by Scott Cook. At $18 million in annual sales, Intuit was a miniature software company compared to Microsoft, which would hit $1 billion in sales in 1990.

Jeff Raikes, the director of Microsoft's applications marketing division informed Cook that Microsoft would be interested in buying his company out and would he be interested in that? He was very interested and the two companies started preliminary talks. It was a company that owned an industry standard and Quicken was outselling its closest competitor six times over, but Chairman Bill decided that the deal was too high and instead proposed an arrangement in which Microsoft and Intuit would work together to develop a join finance management tool. With Microsoft's nationwide distribution channels and market connections, Cook decided that it was too good a deal to pass.

Under this new deal, Intuit would have to share its Quicken source code with Microsoft's applications programmers. *No problem, we are partners*. But as soon as Microsoft had looked under the hood and figured Quicken out, it was no longer interested in the partnership.

In a meeting with Microsoft head of applications Mike Maples, Cook was informed that the company was coming out with its own product and had decided against licensing the Quicken brand name. Microsoft was marketing its own financial management product in one year. This little bit of manipulative conduct and theft of ideas would, like every other sneaky deed, come to bite Microsoft and Bill Gates in the backside.

Chapter 11: Windows 3.0 and the FTC investigation

The decision to break rank with IBM on Windows was not an easy one. Winning the contract to produce MS-DOS for the IBM PC had been the turning point of Microsoft. Bill had always been deferential towards IBM, sometimes to the chagrin of his executives. His decision to shift Microsoft's efforts from Windows and DOS to Presentation Manager had led to the departure of Scott MacGregor who had played a huge part in developing the first version of Windows.

If the partnership with IBM in 1980 had been the turning point for Microsoft, breaking ranks with Big Blue would be their passage to adulthood. And Windows would be the litmus test to determine their mettle. Two versions had already been released to a muted response. Windows 3.0 was supposed to be the capper; an indication of the kind of products the software industry could hope to see coming out of Redmond.

Windows 3.0 was unveiled in a glitzy event in New York City. Bill Gates, the face of Microsoft, was taking point on the unveiling event. The all top brass and senior executives at Microsoft were in attendance and in branches all over the world, employees followed proceedings via satellite. It was a very good bit of software engineering, but that was not the only reason why Windows 3.0 was creating such a huge buzz. At the launch of Windows 1.0, constant delays had made software companies doubt it long before it was unveiled. An operating system cannot do well if there are no applications to go with it.

Like the good student he had always been, Bill had learned from his previous mistakes. Prior to the unveiling of Windows, he had convinced major software companies to come up with applications for Windows. Officially, Microsoft overtook Lotus as the largest software company in America in 1987 when its sales eclipsed those of Lotus. Now Lotus was at the launch of a product that Bill Gates hoped would propel his company to great new heights and they had committed to spend a few million dollars to create applications for Windows 3.0. Lotus could not afford to miss out on the Windows market at a time when Excel was eroding its dominance in the spreadsheet market.

A serious promotional campaign was launched to promote Windows 3.0, including television appearances by Chairman Bill. Shipments hit one million just four months after the glitzy unveiling. No other software product had ever sold as fast and the whole industry was in awe. Bill Gates' decision to break ranks with IBM and push his own product was being rewarded with unprecedented success. In the end, it turned out that Microsoft and IBM were right about there being an OS of the 1990s. They were just wrong about what OS it would be.

IBM was not happy. The runaway success of Windows 3.0 had rendered the OS/2 redundant. The success of Windows almost assuredly meant that OS/2 would not pick up enough users to become an important operating system. At 1% market share to 66% for the DOS in 1989, the situation only got worse when DOS was boosted by the highflying Windows GUI.

To strike back, IBM entered into the Patriot Partnership with Metaphor Computer Systems in a venture that would produce OS-fluid software. This meant that programmers did not need to go through Microsoft to receive technical support to create software. If successful, the venture would also reduce the dominance of DOS due to a glut of application software for the operating system and give other operating systems, for which applications had not been created, a chance to compete with Microsoft. If such a platform could be created, it would be a silver bullet to Microsoft. One of the reasons why Windows and DOS were doing so well was because Bill Gates had spent years promoting it to software companies and wheedling them to write application software for it.

But the partnership was facing serious problems because Bill did not get along with Jim Cannavino, IBM's new chairman. Nor did he agree with the way IBM was run. The last few meetings with Jim had left him raving in outrage at what he called Jim's attempts to dictate to him how to run Microsoft. Evidence of this would come out in an explosive InfoWorld expose in September 1990, long after Windows 3.0 had been released. But the seed had been planted about four months previously.

During the 1990 Computer Bowl at the Boston World Trade Center, Bill got together for a few drinks with a few Lotus employees. Despite the fierce rivalry between the two giants for the top spot in personal computer software, employees were often in friendly terms. Bill had met with George Gilbert, a huge fan of his, in 1989. Bill had gone on to offer him a job at Redmond, but George preferred to stay in Boston. For the evening out with Chairman Bill, George invited a handful of employees. They all wanted to pick the brain of the man who literary had the personal computing industry in the palm of his hands.

But Bill was not interested in talking business. In an exceptionally rare moment of candor, he kept his audience enthralled not with his insights on the future of the computer industry, but a monologue on his own life. Among these strangers he hardly knew and would probably never meet again, Bill poured his heart out.

He defended the decision to develop a 16-bit version of OS/2 because it strengthened the Microsoft/IBM partnership. Even though the operating system had performed dismally in the market, he still had hopes that it would pick up. That could only happen when Microsoft stopped holding back on fixing bugs on the next generation of OS/2, but IBM was not encouraging them to abandon their more successful Windows and DOS for OS/2 and Presentation Manager. He expressed confidence that his company's products would win hands down over IBM's, but he was also dismayed that external forces were souring the partnership.

In a flight of what may be considered arrogance but is really clear-headed thinking, Bill asserted that Big Blue was more dependent on him than he was on them. After all, his software was dominating the operating systems and applications market. It was a factual truth, but it could not be expected to sit well with the likes of Cannavino at IBM. To add salt to injury, Bill predicted that Big Blue would go out of business in just ten years because of their outdated business practices.

IBM was a huge company with as much bureaucracy as a small country. Things took too long to happen and their innovative edge was a joke. Just look at how things are done at Microsoft! Rather than creating an easy-going environment, Bill had cultivated a cutting edge culture to product innovation by periodically slashing out the bottom 5% in a bi-annual peer review. Working at Microsoft was a privilege that had to be earned and only the best could be retained.

Jim Cannavino had tried to tell Bill how to run Microsoft. Now it was time for Bill Gates to return that favor, just not to him, but to a bunch of Lotus employees whom he barely knew. IBM kept its development teams too big to take advantage of personal input by individual employees. If IBM hoped to produce cutting edge products, maybe they should consider slimming down.

George and his colleagues decided to each write up the events of the evening with Bill to the best of their recollection just for record-keeping sake. It was not every day that a bunch of low-level employees gets to spend the evening with the most powerful man in the industry. George's decision to write out last night's events would turn out to be fatal for Bill Gates. He flew back to Seattle after the Computer Bowl without the slightest idea the events he had set in motion in his bar-side chat with George and his colleagues.

Four months later, George Gilbert's zeal to immortalize the words of his hero would have a cataclysmic effect. After writing down his recollections of the evening with Bill Gates, he had decided to write a memo and send it to his superiors too. He was hoping that the company's top brass might learn from the insightful views of Chairman Bill since Lotus happened to be heavily invested in OS/2 applications.

It turned out that its relationship with IBM was a more important aspect of their future plans, or their rivalry with Microsoft was an even bigger priority. George was just a lower mid-level executive at Lotus, so it took a while for the memo to reach Lotus chairman Jim Manzi. Manzi then sent it to IBM chairman Cannavino and being a former journalist himself, probably the media.

InfoWorld broke the story in September 1990 just when the relationship between Microsoft and IBM was at its lowest ebb. And so the world received their first look into the deepest reaches of Bill Gates' psyche; the man who always steered the conversation back to Microsoft when journalists asked about his life was naked and on display for the whole world to see.

Bill Gates' scandalous assertions turned out to be the last straw to a relationship on the rocks. In just one week following the article, IBM was solely in charge of OS/2 and Microsoft was freed from its obligations to develop OS/2. In the end, Windows 3.0 turned out to be the ultimate Microsoft product in more ways than one; the best-selling operating system, the industry standard, and the product that ended their partnership with IBM. Through Windows, Microsoft became not the company that was lucky enough to score the IBM software contract, but the start-up that had broken away from IBM and came out of the other side the better for it. InfoWorld's article was nothing a competent public relations team could not repair in time.

In fact, the only serious damage that came out of the revelations made by George Gilbert's memo was the accusations that Microsoft had misled the software industry into investing in OS/2 while Microsoft focused development efforts on Windows. Microsoft had a huge advantage in application software as a result. These accusations added to existing accusations of antitrust practices by Microsoft.

Windows 3.0 had carved out a niche market with 1 million copies sold in the first four months, but Bill was still promoting it long after InfoWorld had released the damming memo. In the 1990 fall Comdex, he continued pushing Windows as the new industry standard, speaking out on the advantages of having just one operating system to run applications on; the essence of his "a computer on every desk and Microsoft software on every computer" motto.

In 1990, the whole world was still marveling at the internet, a 1986 invention that was just picking steam. Little business utility had been created for the internet, but Bill had a hunch that the internet would soon make the computer a state-of-the-art access point for information. At this point, however, he had not figured out a way for Microsoft to capitalize on this exciting new invention.

A month later, like two exes trying to make it work as friends after breaking up, IBM and Microsoft announced a joint venture to come up with multimedia applications for the personal computer. They were joined in this undertaking by other computer manufacturers (to make it less weird that they were hanging out together) but the tensions were still high between the two companies.

But trouble for Microsoft was blowing from an entirely different direction. Microsoft had squared off with dozens of companies in the computer industry and won. Most of these showdowns had occurred behind the closed doors of boardrooms and executive offices involving lesser players. And if Microsoft could square off against the bluest of the blue chip companies (IBM) and inflict as much damage as it had done, the damage to smaller firms would be even more fatal. There were claims that he suppressed innovation to prevent new entrants from growing strong enough to challenge

Microsoft.

Company executives who had done business revealed that Bill would do anything to win regardless of the cost of that victory to the opponent or the industry as a whole. An executive took exception with Bill's bigger-than-life demeanor and market domination that forced every software company to defer to Microsoft on any strategic decision. With such animosity directed towards Microsoft, it was just a matter of time before someone went and snitched on them, getting them an adversary who would shake them to the core. In the end, a Utah-based company called WordPerfect that competed with Microsoft Word admitted to having lodged complaints against Microsoft with the Fair Trade Commission.

The Federal Trade Commission started the probe into Microsoft's fair competition violations in June 1990. For almost a whole year, the FTC went through thousands of documents detailing the business practices at Microsoft to determine the magnitude of their antitrust violations. Other apparent monopolies, IBM included, had faced off against the US government. A federal investigation was a death knell that any big company dreaded. In the IBM investigation, the company had become so entangled in litigation that a whole law firm had to be created to help the company avoid being broken down into fragments of the original.

AT&T, the telecommunication giant christened Ma Bell had fared far worse than IBM. At the height of its power, Ma Bell had dominated the telecommunications industry, exercising a monopoly that doomed lesser players to helplessly snapping at its tail. In the end, the company had been broken down into tiny little Baby Bells. One of them, the AT&T mother company had given Microsoft its very first operating system, XENIX. If Microsoft could come out of the antitrust investigation whole, it would join the league of legends. But the attacks on Microsoft were not restricted to the US government machinery. The media was also interested in taking a bite off the scrumptious fruit that was Microsoft in 1990; a successful tech company with trendsetting products that was actively taking on bigger companies and winning.

In early 1991, a magazine called Business Month ran a headline story on its cover asking the question that many people had been asking for a long time. Below a caricature of Bill Gates as a muscleman, the magazine captioned; "The

Silicon Bully: How Long Can Bill Gates Kick Sand in the Face of The Computer Industry?" More than twenty executives in the computer industry were interviewed for the article, which would turn out to be Business Month's last before it went out of business. In this article, every insult was hurled at Microsoft and at Bill, the man who many viewed as the personification of the company. Many of the interviewees declined to put a name to their testimony, probably in fear of retribution.

Following in the wake of Business Month's damning article, the FTC investigation was broken to the public in the afternoon of March 11, 1991. Rick Sherlund, a Goldman Sachs analyst broke the news to media houses informing them that the Federal Trade Commission was looking into Microsoft antitrust violations. The report was followed by a press release by Microsoft the next morning acknowledging the FTC investigation and affirming its cooperation. The press release shed light into the probe; the IBM/Microsoft joint press conference in which they had restated their commitment to OS/2 as an industry standard. The FTC was concerned that the decision by Microsoft to push Windows instead had amounted to collusion to misdirect software companies and pave the way for

Microsoft to win over their competitors by developing software for Windows, their real intended standard.

In a real sense, events transpiring immediately after the press conference had forced Bill Gates to redirect Microsoft internal policy. There was no reason for the company to fear anything because everyone knew the inside version of what really transpired. They could just sit pretty and await the exoneration they knew would soon be coming. Bill Gates even gave an interview to reassure the public and investors that there was nothing to fear. In retrospect, that was a very naïve thing to say. The media had taken the story and run wild with it. The stock market, sensing an impending scandal, wanted nothing to do with Microsoft and its stock nose-dived.

In this volatile environment, all those people with unflattering views about Microsoft had the perfect avenue to voice their misgivings. But even more than Microsoft, one person seemed to be the target of many unflattering remarks; the one man who had singularly shaped the software giant, influenced the corporate culture in the company more than any other employee, and spearheaded their quest to crush competitors and send them out of business. A man who wore huge glasses, was often shabbily dressed, and had a proclivity for yelling at people; Bill Gates.

Some of the most critical quotes from articles and television appearances included a very hostile "I'd like to put an icepick in Gates' head" from the Business Month article. It had been featured in an interview by an unnamed IBM executive; no surprises there, Bill had really taken the two-flusher on them. Another ferocious foe was Mitch Kapor, the man who had founded Lotus Corporation. Reeling from an upset by Bill with the Macintosh software deal of 1985 with Excel and having been overtaken two years later as the biggest software company in the world, Mitch had a mouthful to say about his adversary.

He branded Bill as a traitor who had used all the leverage he had as Microsoft Chairman to crush smaller, more excellent companies, essentially selling out the software industry for market share and personal wealth. He signed off with the ringing declaration that "the (personal computer) revolution is over... the innovation of the software industry has ended... it's the Kingdom of the Dead."

As an old friend and partner, Mitch Kapor's

statement hurt Bill. "Kingdom of the Dead, really?" he asked. What he didn't know was that all those rivals who had suffered defeat under his strong arm had found their chance to get even. The discontent that had been building in the software and hardware computer industry for ten years came pouring out in a few short months and it was merciless in its indictment of Chairman Bill. While the FTC focused its investigations on malpractices in Microsoft the company, to anyone who had done business with them, the buck stopped at one man only and they tore into him as mercilessly as he had torn into their freedom to do business with Microsoft's competitors or directed product strategy to steal market share from their products.

The voices of his supporters were suppressed, but they were still there. They were also, obviously, less passionate in their defense. Hate usually has more fervor than love or admiration, especially the animosity of a large group of people. One ardent supporter was Gordon Eubanks, president of Symantec who had competed with Microsoft on BASIC. He acknowledged that Bill had used his influence to win, but insisted that anyone in his position would have done the same thing.

And if Mitch Kapor decided to screw his friend over and criticize him in the media, Vern Raburn, another friend, former Microsoft manager, and current competitor had nothing but nice things to say about Bill. According to him, Bill was only being bashed because he was the big guy. His competitive ways were just an extension of his winning mentality, and his victories over competitors was not an indication of ill-will, just that winning nature that made him a formidable competitor himself.

In the meantime, the FTC was realizing that Microsoft's misdoings stretched further than the 1989 Comdex press briefing. The probe was extended to cover anti-competitive practices throughout its young history. The media eagerly published and aired stories of people who had been upset by Microsoft and soon enough, the line between Microsoft bashing and Bill bashing had grown microscopic. In his defense, Bill insisted that he did not care about money, as everyone claimed. He was singularly focused on winning and taking his company to the highest levels of success he could. And it was all true. Unfortunately, that was not the issue in question.

The FTC unearthed the details about the Intuit attempted merger and eventual screw-over in

October 1990. Microsoft Money, the product of Microsoft's antics the previous year, was announced about one month after Scott disclosed the events surrounding Microsoft's attempted merger in 1989 to the FTC. He insisted that he did not bear any ill-will towards Microsoft or Bill Gates. Bill was simply being a good manager, sizing up rivals and scouting for new avenues to bring new business into the company. Cook was enough of a sportsman to defend Bill Gates and blast the companies that had allowed him to one-up them in a way similar to Microsoft's appropriation of his Quicken idea. In his opinion, Bill Gates' antics were just a product of his high intelligence and competitive nature. He did not see anything wrong with it. He was a lone voice.

Despite Scott Cook's lack of animosity and actual defense of Bill Gates, his testimony (and that of other companies that had suffered the same fate as him) prompted the FTC to widen their probe. Microsoft's control of operating systems, application software, and computer peripherals constituted a monopoly the FTC would have to try and take down. The testimony offers came pouring into the FTC as executives lined up to pour their hearts out about the big bad that was now Microsoft and Chairman Bill. The commission took testimonies about price undercutting, attempts to block companies from accessing the market, and of course the good old plagiarism of ideas.

The boy who had grown up competing in grownup sports and holding his own had grown up to become a formidable competitor in so many fields it was incredible how he managed to win in all of them. That the losers would come back to try and get him back for it was less of a surprise. And Bill Gates was not a competitor who believed in backing down. Doubling up was more his thing.

In fact, it appears like the FTC investigation and industry-wide condemnation only sharpened his predatory ways. All through the 1990s, an ever-expanding line-up of companies came out with complaints that Microsoft had screwed them over. The grievances all followed the same trajectory. Microsoft would spot a company with a great product and approach it for a partnership. After learning all they needed to learn about it, they would put together a team of developers and release a competing product.

Whatever his nonchalant reaction to it, there would be hell to pay if the FTC found Microsoft guilty of engaging in monopolistic activities and Bill Gates, though outwardly unconcerned, was growing concerned. As the FTC and seemingly everyone in the personal computer industry ganged up against him, his veneer of invincibility cracked. The world was treated to a front row seat to watch the weakness in a leaked state-of-the-company confidential memo in the spring of 1991. It would come to be known as the 'nightmare memo,' a candid missive that showed to the whole world that Bill Gates was indeed motivated by the fear of failure in all his business dealings.

For the past few years, a storm of dire proportions and great destructive power had been gathering speed and it now reared its head at Microsoft and everything the company stood for. If Apple were to win their lawsuit and succeed in getting the courts to stop Microsoft using the GUI, all its star products would be illegal. There was simply no way Microsoft could survive losing Windows, Excel, Word, and other products that had been raking in the dollars for their bank reserves. Furthermore, a win by Apple would also see Microsoft fined $4 billion, a hefty amount that the company could not possibly hope to survive. These products were receiving a thumping from smaller, more responsive software companies that were beating Microsoft's product in its own Windows OS. The worst case scenario of being indicted in the FTC was the breaking up of Microsoft's division into constituent companies. The company could not survive such an operation. Its strength lay in the interdependence between divisions, its diversity being its greatest asset.

The memo sent the media into a tailspin of newspaper articles and television broadcasts peppered with a healthy dose of speculation and damnation. The Microsoft stock experienced its biggest ever plummet in the face of Microsoft's vulnerability- 6.6% in just one day's trading. The fact that Bill Gates and not just any analyst had made the assertions to his company's vulnerability lent great credence to these fears. Personally, Bill lost a whopping $315 million on paper.

It was sheer luck that another distressed memo leaked to the media soon after his. This time, it originated from John Akers, the then IBM Chairman. He was seething at continued loss of market share by IBM that had culminated in a second straight decline in annual sales. Suddenly, Microsoft's ominous future did not appear like such an isolated case. However, the foe it would now have to face was as unprecedented as anything could get in the personal computer industry.

Ever since IBM had entered the PC market with its IBM personal computer, Big Blue had had to contend with the might of Apple Computers, a pioneering computer company that had started in a garage that was nonetheless setting trends. But desperate situations call for desperate measures and the rivalry with Microsoft was turning into a desperate situation. John Akers decided to execute a maneuver that would take the whole computer industry by storm; an alliance with Apple. Apple was another computer company that had found itself in a tight spot, also caused by the maneuvering of Microsoft. The two needed each other if they were to survive the tempest times and take down a common foe. Both had danced the tango with Microsoft and hurt each other's performance in the retail market. It could even be argued that Microsoft was losing on two fronts by the mere announcement of an IBM/Apple alliance. Sales of Excel and Word, two of the companies more successful consumer applications, relied heavily on their licensing agreements with Apple.

When the IBM/Apple alliance was announced, it shook the computer industry to the core. For all other computer manufacturers, the prospect of facing off to the might of Big Blue and the ingenious innovation of Apple was a scary prospect. Why, the two were big enough adversaries alone! Together, they would sweep the market from right under their feet. But if Compaq and Digital Equipment had reasons to tremble at the prospect of an IBM/Apple alliance, Microsoft had more reason to fear it. Big Blue was still eyeing the software market that had been their bread and butter for a decade and a half now and Apple was even then suing Microsoft for the very foundation of their future; GUI technology. It was a desperate situation alright.

Another alliance would have to be forged. Microsoft joined ranks with Compaq and Digital Computers in an alliance of their own. They brought into the fold another 18 companies who stood to lose market share if IBM went ahead to produce a standard for PCs. The new alliance christened themselves the Advanced Computing Environment. They could always find safety in numbers and they found it in the Reduced Instruction Set Computing (RISC) computer standard. ACE would be the ace Microsoft needed to stand up to the IBM/Apple alliance... and probably strengthen its position in the software industry.

IBM and Apple were also targeting the RISC microchip to stand up to Microsoft's bullying and get their respective products off the slump in which they were both stuck. Another ulterior motive IBM had in courting Apple was to mitigate any damage to their OS/2 operating system should Microsoft lose its rights to the graphical user interface technology they had copied from the Macintosh. The trial was proceeding in federal court and was the pivot that sent Microsoft stock climbing or dropping every time a pre-trial motion was won by either side.

But the IBM/Apple alliance was more reactionary than anything else. The two companies were so different in their corporate cultures that it was doubtful that they could come up with any real products. So Microsoft was not exactly trembling in fear. In fact, some executives expressed relief in the knowledge that their long involvement was finally coming to a disastrous end.

Bill Gates went as far as calling the alliance ill-fated, especially for Apple. He told the Wall Street Journal as much, stating that Apple had "sold its birthright" by joining ranks with IBM." And in a way he was right. The company had built its reputation on its ability come up with unique products and setting standards that no other company (except perhaps Microsoft) could replicate. On the other hand, IBM-compatibility had made the IBM PC as unique as cotton candy in a children's party. Interestingly enough, many Apple employees agreed with him.

It is quite possible that Apple was simply struggling with its corporate direction after the ousting of founder and former CEO Steve Jobs six years before. John Sculley, the man popular for stating that Apple was a marketing company rather than a tech one, was bleeding the company dry with his ineptitude. He would be replaced at the helm by Michael Spindler in 1993, who in turn attempted to turn around the dimming fortunes of Apple and only succeeded in sending it hurtling towards bankruptcy. It wasn't until Steve Jobs returned to the company that Apple returned to its former winning ways.

As it were, the IBM/Apple alliance would soon prove to be a hopeless partnership when the fall Comdex rolled around and IBM failed to introduce its OS/2 as it had announced. No one at Microsoft had expected the announcement to really happen and they were all thrilled. Steve Ballmer was saved knowing what it would be like to digest a floppy disk, as he had promised to do if IBM had managed to get OS/2 ready to ship by the fall Comdex.

While IBM reported losses totaling $2.8 billion, the company's first shortfall in its long and glorious history, and the financial situation at Apple remained stagnant, Microsoft announced its most successful year yet. Microsoft (and Bill Gates) was vindicated. The Microsoft stock enjoyed a resurgence that sent Bill Gates and his band of share-owning top executives into great new heights in personal wealth.

By all indications, Bill had won the long and arduous battle. After prevailing against IBM/Apple and a whole gaggle of rivals he had bested, he would have a very successful and peaceful next few years. Starting in 1992 when President George H. W. Bush awarded him with the National Medal of Technology for his contributions to personal computing. It was also in the year 1992 that he was officially listed as the richest man in the world. This trajectory of awards would be continued in 1994 as Bill was honored as a Distinguished Fellow of the British Computer Society for his contribution to computing; a huge distinction considering that only 19 other men had been inducted into the society before him.

In the main, the year 1993 was Microsoft's year of vindication. In a span of one week in the month of August, the FTC closed its investigations into antitrust practices at Microsoft without taking any prosecutorial actions against the company on August 20th. Four days later, the Apple copyright case was dismissed in federal court.

However, the exoneration was only momentary as Apple Computers appealed the dismissal and the FTC was simply handing over their investigation to the Department of Justice. Their legal problems were far from over. It would be a year before the Apple copyright suit was completely thrown out, but the Department of Justice investigation would continue to haunt the company into the next millennium.

Chapter 12: The Final Years

Back at Microsoft, Bill continued supervising the Windows NT and 95 projects that had been going on at the same time. Windows NT and Windows 95 were part of a genius move in which Bill Gates had decided to start pitting Microsoft products against each other as well as those of their competitors, sharpening the company's competitive edge and increasing its overall market share.

As he sought to increase the already high number of Windows users in the coming years, numerous versions of Windows would be released (sometimes in the same year) until the market was saturated with Windows. He had gotten it right with the fastest-shipping Windows 3.0 in 1990 and since then subscriptions had grown to over 25 million, but Bill wanted to have "Windows on every computer" and he was right on track to achieving this dream. As a result of his efforts, Microsoft was on track to reaching the milestone of being the only software company that has consistently succeeded in putting Windows in over 90% of all personal computers since the later 1990s.

The year 1995 was a busy one for Bill Gates. The company had been doing well since facing off with IBM and Apple three years prior. The Department of Justice was sniffing at their heels, but it was nothing to give them undue concern. Windows was without doubt the industry standard in operating systems. And maybe Chairman Bill had become a little distracted with events in his personal life- an engagement in 1993, planning a wedding all through the year and marrying on New Year's in 1994, then a personal loss with the passing of his mother. So it is really no surprise that Microsoft had mostly missed the internet tidal wave that was sweeping through the world. At the very least, up until mid-1995, he had failed to capitalize on the internet.

Microsoft had been toying with the idea of creating its own web browser since 1994 which had been named Internet Explorer. The World Wide Web had been gaining in popularity since 1993 with browsers like Mosaic and Cello, and Lynx. It would be too late to develop a browser from scratch, so Microsoft decided to license one instead. To find the licensee, Microsoft cast a wide net and at the end it had narrowed the list down to the Netscape Navigator by Spyglass Corporation and BookLink. After preliminary talks with both companies, Microsoft decided to pursue BookLink, which would have allowed the company to own all the company's assets rather than sublicense a base code from the National Center for Supercomputing Applications (NCSA) through Spyglass. However, AOL beat Microsoft to a deal with BookLink, leaving Microsoft out in the cold.

Microsoft reverted back to Spyglass and succeeded in signing a licensing deal in which it would pay a minimum royalty and a share of all added costs to bundle Internet Explorer with its Windows operating system.

In May 26 1995, Bill Gates wrote the "Internet Tidal Wave" memo calling the attention of Microsoft employees to the revolution sweeping through the computer industry with internet applications. He asserted that communications networks would replace software capabilities in computers within 20 years, in essence calling the attention of his employees to the fact that their company would be extinct in 20 years if they did not jump on board with internet applications. By this time, Internet Explorer was just about to start shipping. Even though the "Internet Tidal Wave" memo was not meant for the public and was supposed to be a policy statement for company executives, it raised great publicity for Microsoft and paved the way for the release of IE.

This was the beginning of Bill Gates efforts to have Microsoft place greater emphasis on the internet. In the memo, he intimated that he believed the internet would grow to be bigger than the graphic user interface that had brought Windows to the Microsoft brand. GUI was simply a means to an end, but the internet had the capacity to become an end, with countless applications in multimedia content, communication, and numerous other applications. A computer without the internet may be used to create documents or perform numerous other tasks. Internet connectivity transformed it into a workstation that could allow people to work exclusively on their computers. In his 'computer on every desk and Microsoft software on every computer' vision, Bill envisioned a future in which computers would replace paper. The internet would enable him to achieve this dream.

The direction of Microsoft would be changed dramatically with that one memo. Bill Gates believed that internet environments and networks would be the growth industry of the new millennium. The Internet Explorer project was not receiving the urgency it deserved as the future of Microsoft. But with Bill personally supervising works on the IE, it was ready to ship in the fall of 1995, just three months behind Windows 95. Windows 95 was selling well, but not much better than earlier hits like Windows 3.0. IE was just the thing to boost sales and announce Microsoft's arrival to the browser industry.

A fall Comdex assured Microsoft of a wide immediate audience- up to 90,000 attended the conventions. Rather than sell it as a stand-alone product, Microsoft decided to bundle it up with Windows 95 as a free special add-on package. Customers who had already installed Windows 95 could get the add-ons through service packs. The inclusion of IE sent Windows 95 shooting into the stratosphere. By 1996, Windows 95 had sold more than 25 million copies.

Giving Internet Explorer away for free was a return to the old questionable competitive practices for which the company had been investigated by the FTC. Spyglass made significantly less money in royalties than it would have made had Microsoft actually charged its customers for IE. In addition to the loss of royalties, Spyglass was quickly losing market share to Internet Explorer. So in a way, licensing their base code for Microsoft to create IE was double jeopardy for Spyglass.

This period when Microsoft's Internet Explorer competed with Spyglass 'Netscape Navigator would later be christened the "first browser wars" period. As usual, Microsoft played it dirty. Cheating Spyglass millions in potential earnings in royalties by giving IE free was one way of doing this. It was a beautifully designed strategy that allowed them to kill two birds with one stone; free IE to its large customer base increased its market share to the peril of Netscape Explorer and no money in royalties weakened the financial muscle of Spyglass to compete.

As a break-away company from the NCSA, formed by developers of the first browser in the world named Mosaic, royalty earnings was an important source of revenue for Spyglass. Having received the bare minimum in royalties from Microsoft all through 1995, Spyglass was hurting. To protest, the company threatened to have Microsoft audited to determine how much money in royalties it was owed. The dispute was settled in early 1997 with an $8 million settlement split into $7.5 million in cash and $500,000 in software concessions.

All through the second half of the 1990s, Microsoft was in software and computer peripherals as well as the browser market. A few years before, Microsoft had gone head to head with IBM for the control of PC software and come out strong while IBM recorded serious losses. The time was ripe for Microsoft to measure itself against another rival- Spyglass. Incidentally, this rival, just like IBM, had started as a partner; Microsoft had licensed Mosaic base code from Spyglass to create Internet Explorer.

No worthy competitor challenged Microsoft's dominance in the personal computer software market but in the internet access applications market, Internet Explorer 2.0, which happened to be doing really well in the browser market, faced serious opposition from Netscape Navigator. Tactics like the bundling together of IE (a source of revenue for both companies) with Windows hurt revenues for Microsoft.

But Bill was willing to endure the loss of revenue for now if it would bring him glory in the long run. After all, Microsoft was a billion dollar company that could afford to lose millions in potential revenues. Spyglass could not. Gradually, the fact that Internet Explorer was a genuinely good browser, coupled with tireless behind-the-scenes machinations, allowed it to pull ahead of the competition. The market share commanded by IE peaked at over 90% in 2004.

The browser wars period, a popular story in the internet access community, proved that Bill still had the capacity to take on the biggest, most invincible rival and prevail. His uncompromising anything-goes view of competition, while hurtful to other companies, had proved extremely effective once again.

Meanwhile, on the build-up to the browser wars, Microsoft was seeking alternative investment opportunities to diversify their income streams. In 1995, the company entered into a strategic partnership with the National Broadcasting Corporation (NBC) to develop a pay-cable TV channel named MSNBC. Microsoft would provide the technical support and online broadcast services while NBC was responsible for bringing content to the screen. The channel was launched officially in July 15th 1996. The online news service was good for IE as it gave users the option to receive news right through their desktops or other Microsoft enabled devices.

The internet was becoming an astoundingly important part of Microsoft's future outlook as intended in Bill Gates' 1995 "Internet tidal wave" memo. Not even with GUI had Bill Gates been so passionate about an innovation. The development of Internet Explorer would go down in history as Microsoft's most intensively funded project. The deal with MSNBC also allowed the company to control a news website where innovations in browsing interfaces might be tested. These kinds of investments in which the internet was simply a small package in a bigger product would be the strategy through which internet use would be extended to more people. As the dominant player in the browsing market as well as the operating software market, any promotion on these two industries was an indirect promotion of Microsoft.

Bill Gates' conviction on role of the internet to the future of humanity was so huge that he wrote a book about it. In November 1995, the book *The Road Ahead*, written with Microsoft Chief Technology Officer Nathan Myhrvold, and Peter Rinearson, was published by Viking Penguin Publishers. In the book, Bill expressed the belief that he considered the internet as the most remarkable advancement in the personal computer industry since the IBM PC. He also voiced his concerns that the internet was still a long way from the information highway it could be. Even though the book was well received and spent 7 weeks on the New York Times bestseller list, the quote was an embarrassing lack of vision for the Microsoft CEO.

The internet had exploded into critical mass usage in the few months between writing the book and publishing it. Bill Gates had grossly underestimated the growth of the internet. He immediately embarked on a new updated version that put to account the explosive growth of internet use in America. Rather than being an autobiography detailing the life of Bill Gates- at that time the richest man in the world- the book focused on the future, which in 1995 Bill Gates firmly believed to be the internet. But like any other large company, diversification was a means of survival the company simply could not ignore.

Microsoft had broken the record for $1 billion in annual revenues back in 1990. By 1998, the company's capital reserves were in excess of $5 billion. Investing this money in promising companies seemed like a better use of resources than letting the money lay around in a bank. The Executive Committee voted to invest in Comcast, building on the company's portfolio of television-related investments. The company's internet applications division received a boost too with the acquisition of a stake in RealNetworks, a streaming video company. Microsoft did not commit to go hard for this market though, else they might have formed a Netflix-like company ten years before video streaming became a global industry.

A year after Steve Jobs had been re-installed at Apple after his ousting twelve years before, Bill led Microsoft to invest in Apple too. With Steve Jobs at the helm, Microsoft's relationship with Apple was good enough for Apple to go into a partnership to create Windows 1998 for Mac. Bill Gates obviously had a connection with Steve Jobs that allowed the two companies to partner that Sculley had not had.

Even though Bill Gates remained to be associated with Microsoft, he was heading towards a time when he would be devoting his life entirely to the Bill and Melinda Gates Foundation. The new software continued doing what Microsoft does- set standards. For example, an Interactive Media division was created to develop multimedia applications for Windows, increasing the utility of computers in general and building a new selling point for Windows OS. The time was nearing when Bill would have to vacate his executive office for good. To strengthen the senior leadership of the company and lessen the responsibilities shouldered by the office of the CEO, Bill Gates reorganized leadership at the highest levels of Microsoft, appointing an Executive Committee to replace the Office of the President. The more decentralized leadership allowed the company to strengthen its products and increase the overall profitability of Microsoft.

Having more decentralized leadership also allowed Bill to gradually distance himself from the day-to-day operations of the company. Having spent twenty years practically breathing Microsoft, Bill Gates was slowly paving the way for him to leave the company and join his wife in charity work. But before he could separate himself from Microsoft he would have to face his greatest nightmare once again. This time around, the Department of Justice, the investigative authority that had taken over the Microsoft antitrust probe from the FTC in 1993, had joined rank with 20 US states and the District of Columbia to prosecute Microsoft for unfair competition practices.

The year before, the Department of Justice concluded the decade-long investigation into anti-trust business tactics at Microsoft. It was time now for Bill Gates to face the music. In the trial, Bill Gates gave testimony that was considered by many people to be evasive, refusing to directly take responsibility for many business policies that were enforced during his time as Chairman, CEO, and President, and some while he held just two of the titles. Until

2000, Bill Gates had held two or more of the senior-most positions in the company. All evidence submitted during the trial pointed to him being aware and approving of decisions that amounted to monopolistic practices. The judge ordered Microsoft broken into separate operating systems and application software divisions.

Microsoft promptly filed an appeal at the Supreme Court and subsequently won in the district circuit court of appeals where the Supreme Court had referred the case. The trial would stretch all the way to late 2001 when the Department of Justice withdrew its application for Microsoft to be split up. A few months later, the trial was settled out of court. The cloud that had momentarily threatened the future of Bill Gates' life work had been lifted. By the time the settlement was arrived at, Bill Gates was no longer at the helm.

Bill vacated the position of company CEO in 2000, bequeathing the office to Ballmer and only retaining his position as chairman of the board and chief software architect. An interesting position to hold because it took him full cycle back to his time as an avid programmer before forming Microsoft and being drawn into the business end of operations. While he still checked over the code and made changed in the 1980s, it was becoming harder to do the same with Microsoft's multi-layered office environment in the 1990s. As chief software architect, Bill Gates was going back to where it all started and leaving the more business-oriented operations of the office of the CEO to Ballmer, the business school graduate.

Despite the negative publicity brought about by the high-profile trial, Bill Gates was named CEO of the year 1999 after winning a poll conducted by the Chief Executive Officer Magazine. In fact, the trial was so immaterial to the opinions of the market on the health of Microsoft that the stock rose to greater new heights, making Bill Gates reach the mind-blowing net worth of $100 billion for a brief period in 1999. The award was well-timed as it turned out to be the final year of his eligibility.

More personal recognition would follow the 1999 CEO of the year as Bill Gates was listed in the Sunday Times most powerful persons in the world list. The New York Institute of Technology also awarded him the President's Medal for his contribution to technological advancements in the field of computer technology.

In his last few years at the helm of Microsoft, Bill Gates started the slow divestment of authority in the running of the company. He started to delegate important tasks to Steve Ballmer and other members of the Executive Committee. He was training them to run the business when he was no longer around to oversee the day to day operations. Bill Gates retired as Microsoft CEO in the year 2000 and left the company completely in 2006. The only position he would hold in Microsoft henceforth would be that of a chief software architect, the duties he had performed as product strategist since the 1980s, and of course, chairman of the Microsoft executive board.

Chapter 13: Leaving Microsoft and Legacy

Bill Gates' claim to fame at the turn of the century was his role in the formation of the world's biggest computer software company. He had trounced stronger rivals than he by outmaneuvering them and outworking them, driven by the singular objective to power a computing revolution.

In his last few years in charge of software development, Bill Gates displayed an affinity towards corporate social responsibility as the chief software architect. As the reliance on internet applications grew, he realized the need for more secure browsing environments, which could only be achieved by ensuring the highest security integrity of all software products to cushion users from hacking and other forms of intrusion, a growing pain around 2002.

Bill Gates worked on initiatives to improve Microsoft's reliability as a software company and improve the user experience derived by customers. The .NET and Trustworthy Computing are two of the most prominent corporate responsibility projects embarked on by Microsoft to secure online environments and increase the utility of Microsoft software.

In .NET, Microsoft created an environment for the development of web based programs through a large public library of programming languages for flexibility. The .NET Initiative received Apple capital backing by Microsoft, even though it was not a resource-generating product.

On Trustworthy Computing, Bill Gates closed up development works on Windows Vista for a total of 10 weeks to give extensive training to programmers on security protocols for operating systems and application software. The trustworthy computing initiative was built on .NET principles and intended as a tool to give software and internet applications users the confidence that they are in a secure environment.

The move was meant to introduce more security protocols in the base code of Microsoft products, protecting user data from falling into the wrong hands. Internet Explorer was especially vulnerable due to its rising popularity as the world's most popular browser after trouncing Netscape Navigator. In 2004, IE would reach its highest levels of popularity yet- a 90% usage in the market. But entry into the market by companies focused solely on the business of internet browsing, would start eroding the company's market share. However, Internet Explorer may be one project that Microsoft did not mind losing. At its height, the browser required 1,000 programmers to work on maintaining it around the clock and cost the company $100 million a year to keep it running.

As the internet had been growing in popularity and simplifying lives for businesses and people from all over the world, the willingness to shut down operations to enhance security in such a high profile company was a huge boost to security protocols for the whole industry.

The 2000s were a fast-paced period for Microsoft. Despite the increasing considerations to corporate responsibilities, or maybe due to increasing consideration to responsible business practices rather than simply going for the kill, Microsoft's dominance was somehow reduced. The market share of hitherto dominant Internet Explorer had practically been wiped out by new entrants Firefox and Google Chrome within a few years between 2003 and 2005. The loss in market share would continue until IE commanded just a tiny share of the rising surfing population.

However, the lost market share in browsers applications would be reclaimed from an entirely new product. In 2002, Bill Gates led Microsoft in entering the video game console market with the release of Xbox. While the first Xbox gaming set was outsold by more established video game console makers like Sony and Nintendo, it still managed to sell over 20 million game consoles, a very competitive number indeed. On its very first foray into a new and established hardware market since the SmartCard, the company has managed to hold its own. When the Xbox 360 was released two years later, it outsold Sony and Nintendo with a comfortable margin. In five years of selling, the Xbox 360 had sold a total of 40 million units. Kinect, a new innovative peripheral that was released in 2011, sold more than 100,000 units a day when it was launched- the first time a product had been so anticipated and well received.

The department has also been responsible for bringing new trends into video gaming with innovations like the Kinect, which at its release in 2011 was the fastest selling consumer electronics product ever produced. This ability of Microsoft to enter a new market and upset the competition speaks volumes about its foundations as an ambitious software company by two scruffy nerds.

And to cap a long and successful career as a programmer and business manager, Windows would be running on about 95% of computers by the turn of the first decade of the century.

The antitrust monster continued to haunt Microsoft only this time overseas. The European Union fined the company $613 million for antitrust practices involving the inclusion of a media player in Windows. The suit also ordered the media player application removed. Four years later, another fine was imposed, this time amounting to $1.3 billion.

However, the age of Bill Gates at Microsoft was fast approaching its end. After overseeing the new software department at Microsoft for six years while at the same time working in the Bill & Melinda Gates Foundation, Bill Gates started considering a transition to full-time philanthropy around 2006. He announced his intention to retire from Microsoft employment in two years. He made the decision amid increasing demands on his work as a trustee and co-chair at the foundation, which by 2006 was worth over $30 billion. A strategy to generate money for the foundation's activity had been emerging in which donations would sometimes be given in the form of venture investments in social enterprises.

In 2008, Microsoft's longest serving employee finally left the company when Bill Gates' name was struck off the employment register. While still entitled to his chairman gratuity, Bill officially ceased being an employee of Microsoft at this point. His duties as the strategic product manager would be taken over by Ray Ozzie and Craig Mundie in short and long term product strategy respectively. As of 2008, Bill Gates was a full-time worker at his foundation.

With his reputation and influence growing in the media, Bill Gates was involved in an advertisement campaign for the company. The ads featured him and Jerry Seinfeld buying shoes from a discount shoe store where a salesman is trying to sell Bill a pair of shoes that's too big for him. He and Jerry discuss shoes while eating churros, but really they are promoting Microsoft as the future of computing. You don't get it till the very end, but it was a goofy, interesting clip.

Six years after his retirement from day-to-day Microsoft employment, Bill Gates left the company completely when he vacated the office of the chairman of Microsoft. He was succeeded by John W. Thompson, a former IBM vice-president and Symantec CEO. The complete exodus from Microsoft came even as Bill Gates had been divesting his Microsoft stock in the past few years. He no longer owned the largest share of Microsoft stock- the distinction belonged to Steve Ballmer as of 2014- the year of Bill's retirement from the Chairmanship position. However, Bill Gates would continue to be technology advisor to newly appointed CEO Satya Nadella.

Legacy

Bill Gates leaves a more-than-life sized legacy at Microsoft, with milestones including the creation of the first ever BASIC interpreter for the personal computer, a feat of programming genius that spearheaded the personal computer revolution. His Disk Operating System would grow to become the bestselling operating system of the 80s, before the introduction of GUI into the Windows OS, with which the company Bill Gates co-founded would dominate the world PC market with a 90% penetration.

Through Microsoft, Bill Gates would also play a role in popularizing the internet. His 1995 book *The Road Ahead* outlining ways through which the internet would shape the world, reached the number 1 spot on the New York Times bestseller list. Bill Gates' role in the introduction of the internet to the world also includes the browser wars where Microsoft fought with Spyglass for dominance.

Personal achievements in line with Microsoft include obtaining the title of billionaire at the age of 31. This was the result of years of tireless sacrifice, dedication to winning, and a willingness to do anything to win.

For his efforts at Microsoft, Bill Gates has been recognized by the United States government - through the office of the president- and awarded the National Medal of Technology by President H. W. Bush. Bill was also inducted as a Distinguished Fellow of the British Computer Society and awarded with the Bower Award for Business Leadership by The Franklin Institute in 2012. At age 64, Bill Gates is still young and active. The story is yet to come to an end, especially with his business-like brand of philanthropy and innovative ideas. But whatever else he will be known for, Bill Gates' legacy as one of the biggest contributors to computing precedes him.

Also quite admirable is the fact that Bill Gates

once again surpassed the $100 billion net worth mark in 2019. This comes at a time when he has sold many of his Microsoft stock and invested it elsewhere through Cascade Investment, his personal venture capital firm. The Bloomberg Billionaires Index 2013 showed that Bill Gates increased his net worth by $16 billion. A majority of these earnings were from ventures managed through his Cascade Investment outfit.

Established in 1995, Cascade Investments has allowed Bill to put his substantial wealth to profitable use before the time comes to finally divest it along with everything else he owns. In the meantime, however, he seems to be walking in the company of venture capitalists legend Warren Buffett. Bill may be on his way to a reincarnation as a venture capitalist and probably increasing his fortune to great new heights.

His ability to support his charitable efforts while continuing to boost enterprise efforts, such as his investment in TerraPower, a clean energy company is a genius move that indicates that greater things can be expected from Bill Gates.

Chapter 14: Bill Gates the Family Man

In the late 1980s and early 1990's numerous players in the industry as well as Microsoft employees (and their wives) were talking longingly of the time when Bill would finally get married. His competitors like Pete Peterson, an executive vice-president of the company that had set the FTC on Bill's tail, believed that marrying would ease him up and give him something to do other that work.

As for Microsoft employees, the feeling was that Bill neither knew nor appreciated that his employees had families that they needed to spend time with. Microsoft employees worked such ridiculous hours that they never got to spend time with their wives. As a bachelor who wouldn't think twice before sacrificing a relationship for his company, he had driven everyone to work hard, put in ridiculous hours like he did (or at least try), and commit totally to the company.

In 1993, Bill Gates proposed to Melinda French, his girlfriend of six years. She said yes (of course) and the couple took a trip to Africa to celebrate. And unlike other vacations that had given Bill the chance to think up new products for the company, his engagement holiday was spent dreaming up new ways to use his fortune to impact the poverty-ridden world he encountered.

In a TED Talks interview, Melinda Gates said that she discussed with Bill ways through which they could use his vast wealth to improve living conditions for the less fortunate. He was excited by the prospect. His mother had been a dedicated aid-giver; he obviously wanted to follow in her footsteps. The age of combative Bill was coming to an end and would soon be replaced by the more palatable Bill Gates, the world's biggest philanthropist. An idea was born on that vacation: of winning on behalf of the billions of poor people in the world and competing with polio and malnutrition.

A few months after their engagement on New Year's 1994, Bill and Melinda were wedded in a private ceremony inside the golf course of the Manele Bay Hotel, Hawaii. He had gone to great troubles to ensure that no wedding crashers would ruin his marriage, including booking out every room in the hotel.

However, disaster stuck in his personal life when his mother was diagnosed with advanced breast cancer a few months after the wedding. In April 1994, Mary Gates passed away. She was just 65 years old. Her death hit the Gates family hard. Mary had been the lifeblood of the family; organizing Sunday night family dinners, throwing birthday parties, and enforcing a strict attendance policy for thanksgiving and Christmas. The children related with her better than they connected with their father because he had been busy building his career as an attorney in their childhood. Bill Gates had formed a respectful and warm personal friendship with his dad, but it was his mother who had shaped the adult he was; even made him somewhat of a mama's boy, according to some of his exes.

Heartbroken, Bill started to think more seriously about his mother's legacy. She had been an active civic leader, sitting on the boards of several charitable organizations and participating in numerous civic organizations along with her duties as a board member in several billion-dollar Seattle corporations. The one way to honor her memory would be to carry on her charity work. He decided to act on the vision of using his wealth to make an impact in the world.

The widely read Bill Gates had been moved after

reading about the industrialists John D. Rockefeller and Andrew Carnegie. Both Carnegie and Rockefeller had accumulated vast amounts of wealth in their lifetimes, Carnegie in steel and Rockefeller in oil, but by the time of their deaths they had given or were planning to give most of it to charity. This they did by starting charitable organizations. Carnegie wrote the article titled "The Gospel of Wealth" in which he stated his belief that people of great personal wealth have a moral obligation to use their wealth to help others.

Carnegie formed about 7 charitable organizations to carry on his charity work, which was directed towards literacy (by funding the building of libraries throughout the country), scientific research (Carnegie Institution for Science), and education (Carnegie Mellon University) among other causes. John D. Rockefeller followed a more systematic approach to his philanthropy through the Rockefeller Foundation, using the foundation to fund scientific research, education, and healthcare efforts including the near-elimination of yellow fever and hookworm infections in America.

Following in the footsteps of these two giants, Bill made a generous stock donation to start the

William H. Gates Foundation in 1994 with an initial focus of promoting healthcare to poor communities around the world then expanding to promote educational efforts in America and Canada. While he was still held up on the day to day operations of Microsoft, Bill's father spearheaded the foundation's philanthropic activities.

In the year 1996, Melinda Gates left her position as the General Manager of Information Products at Microsoft to focus on raising a family. A year later, she and Bill welcomed their first-born daughter Jennifer Katherine to the world.

Meanwhile, Bill Gates was busy working on a family home for his expanding family. The dream of his ideal house was clear in his mind as far back as 1984 when he had been interviewed about it for a personality profile feature. After breaking ground on a coastal property in 1991, the house was completed about 1995. The house he ultimately built was a 66,000 square feet mansion featuring modern design set in 28 acres of prime land which he had started buying in 1988. Cocooned amidst a copse and opening out to the ocean, the house contained every luxury and security feature a mansion might need, but it also had one of the most advanced smart house system in the world.

Bill Gates had started a whole company – Interactive Home Systems- to support his dream of having an interactive home. He then went on an art-buying spree, purchasing electronic rights to some of the world's best works of arts- like the Codex Leicester among numerous others- to display in the house. Other amenities included a 60-foot swimming pool, a playroom, and indoor theatre. It was a family home fit for the man who had been named the world's youngest billionaire 12 years previously.

In 1998, Bill moved his young family into the new house, just in time for the birth of his second child, son Rory John, in 1999 and three years later, Phoebe Adele.

Family was doing Bill a lot of good. His personality seems to have undergone a shift since his marriage in 1994, becoming less confrontational and not as obsessed with Microsoft as before. While he was the same highly intelligent man with a competitive streak and a matching drive to win, Chairman Bill was slowly transitioning from the full-time Microsoft CEO and Chairman to a husband and philanthropist. And sure, he engineered the browser wars while commuting between his home and the office, but on the whole, he was becoming a more nurturing man and thinking more and more about global issues and how he might solve them than how to take down his competitors at Microsoft.

In 1996, he donated $6 million to Stanford University for the construction of the Gates Computer Science Building, capitalizing on his increasing number of donations towards education causes. Another donation towards educational efforts in this period was made in 1999 to the Massachusetts Institute of Science, giving $20 million for a computer engineering building christened the William H. Gates Building. These projects, while advancing his vision of improving education and using science to solve human problems, were also a boost to his legacy as an outstanding player in the computer industry.

In the early days, flying coach while moving from city to city selling personal computer manufacturers on the vision of Microsoft had been a way to keep himself on edge. He would leave the office a few minutes before take-off to measure Bill Gates against the flight schedule. Then it became a way of life as he set an example for Microsoft executives on keeping costs lean and taking sacrifices for the company.

But the past few years had been getting increasingly difficult for him as he shuffled from one corner of the globe to another on business and coordinating charity efforts for the William H. Gates Foundation. Flying coach was not practical anymore and he needed the flexibility and control that comes from having a private plane to take him wherever his business demanded him to travel. The private jet joined his Porsche as some of what Bill Gates considered his most indulgent luxuries, along with the boat and the Codex Leicester.

The Codex Leicester is a book by Leonardo da Vinci containing his thoughts on scientific principles such as astronomy, fossils, air, celestials, and light. The manuscript is remarkable for having been written in Leonardo's unique mirror style and contains several diagrams and drawings such as that of the Vitruvian man and the helicopter. His purchase of the manuscript for $30 million in 1994 set the record for the highest price a book has ever been sold. Bill Gates has stated in multiple interviews that he was motivated by his fascination for the scientific mind and works of da Vinci to make the purchase.

The manuscript was digitized and has been loaned out to numerous museums around the world for periods of time. Another motivation for buying the book may also have been as part of the interactive media installation for his house. There was also a consideration for Microsoft in the purchase, given that scanned pages of the Codex Leicester have been featured in the Windows 95 and 98 background themes. Bill Gates would always look out for Microsoft.

Even as he raised his three kids, Bill Gates continued to look out for Microsoft. And while even Bill himself admitted that he was not a very engaged parent in the early years, his style of parenting has been observed and discussed in the media since he disclosed that he did not allow his children to own phones till they were 13. The style is described as logic and love and it entails parents communicating with their children on issues, supporting rather than dictating to them, and showing the care and love of parents.

While his children were forbidden from owning phones, Bill remained unshaken in his stand despite their constant complaints that other kids could own a phone. The rule was meant to give the children a chance to experience the world not through the screen of their phones, but through exploration. Of course they could use a friend's phone- and they often did, Bill Gates did not stop them from doing that- but owning a phone was not until they hit their teens.

A phone-free dinner table encourages conversation around the dinner table at the Gates' mansion. This gives Bill and Melinda the time to converse with their children as Bill had done with his parents growing up. This style of limiting their children's access to electronic gadgets is a rising trend among the world's richest tech billionaires. Mark Cuban and Steve Jobs also admitted to restricting the time their children spent playing video games, watching TV, or using their phones.

The children were raised with Catholic beliefs, with Bill stating that he believes religion is an important aspect of personal growth because it shapes our views of the world and our relationship with other people. Even though Bill has never been a habitual churchgoer, he does participate in Catholic mass from time to time. Melinda is the most religious of the couple and introduced the kids to church from a very young age.

Bill and Melinda Gates sought to cultivate the

reading culture in their children by reading to them every day before bed. In a Business Magazine interview, the two disclosed that they had read to their children from books like *Fahrenheit 451* and *Guess How Much I Love You*. Bill Gates confesses that his wife played a bigger role in raising their three children, but he has pitched in where he could over time although mostly his role in the family does appear to be as an authority figure. Melinda is the undisputed head of the family, helping Bill with things like finding the time to talk with his children. In a 2017 Reddit post, he said that Melinda had given him the idea to spend time with the kids by driving them to school, which apparently he wouldn't otherwise have figured out on his own.

In a precedent-setting decision, Bill and his wife Melinda decided that they would leave only $10 million for their children as an inheritance with the rest going to charity. The reasoning behind this move is to ensure that the children make a life for themselves and do not rely on their parent's money. Bill is a firm believer of empowering his children to make a life for their own and supports them every way possible. To provide his first-born daughter with the comfort she needs while pursuing her career as an equestrian, the Gates' went as far as purchasing a house in Florida for her to use whenever she is visiting the city's showjumping facilities or participating in a tournament.

Bill was pleased to attend his daughter's graduation party at Harvard in 2017, the same place from which he had dropped out forty years before but graduated with an honorary degree ten years previously. Jennifer had followed the same footsteps taken by her father in his education: she attended the same Lakewood School where her father had developed his passion for programming and met Microsoft co-founder Paul Allen, as well as a dozen other people who had been instrumental to the establishment of Microsoft as the dominant force in personal computer software it grew to become.

None of the children were ever pressured to join Microsoft. In fact, the idea of hereditary inheritance of the company seemed to be furthest from Bill Gates' mind as he planned his gradual exit from the company from retiring as CEO in 2000 to leaving the chairmanship in 2014. His continued divestment of Microsoft shares indicates that Bill is over his programming days. The children have the freedom to choose their careers without any influence from their parents.

On the whole, Bill Gates is easily one of the most enigmatic people in modern history. His story of unprecedented success against stacked odds is an inspiration to nerds everywhere even though Bill has taken exception to the term in reference to him. He believed that a nerd could not manage people as well as he did, or form and run (quite successfully) a multimillion dollar enterprise. But his nerdy fans did not care that their hero disliked the name.

Even when the powers that be rose against him in the public prosecutions in the 1990s, his supporters staunchly maintained his innocence and even sang his praise. Gilbert, the Lotus employee who got Bill in trouble with his 1990 memo put it best; "Bill Gates... proved (the cause of all nerds) to all the business people who tended to look down on nerds as having no business skills."

First and foremost, Bill Gates is a classic nerd. Maybe not the boring, socially awkward kind that society seems to disparage, although he exhibited social awkward tendencies since he was young. However much he denies it, Bill Gates and his admiration for the technically proficient demonstrates an affinity to people with more intellectual prowess. As far back as during his time at Lakeside, Bill related better to people like him, the computer room gang more than any other student at Lakeside School, because they understood the workings of his mind better than anyone else. As a result of his pickiness in friends, other students branded him high and mighty. These sorts of misrepresentation of character caused trouble for him throughout his life.

A perfect example is with Ed Roberts dealing with Bill's outspoken nature. His parents had encouraged their children to ask questions, so Bill Gates was never afraid to ask the difficult ones which is, pretty much the definition of having a confrontational or combative character. Bill Gates has always been considered combative by pretty much every person who encountered him even before he became a young Microsoft executive. People responded to his outspoken nature in different ways. Some, like Ed Roberts, disapproved and blatantly stated that they preferred a different personality altogether (in Ed Robert's case, the more chilled out Microsoft co-founder Paul Allen).

A competitive streak has always been identifiable in Bill since he was young. Again, this goes back to his upbringing. In the Gates family, every task was a competition from yard games to swimming exercises. Moreover, there was always a tangible reward for winning and a penalty for losing, often having to do chores. For a young child, lounging while a sibling labored away in one chore or another, or doing chores while a sibling lounges about was bound to disposition one towards winning. It is no surprise therefore, that Bill grew up to be so competitive.

Before proposing and marrying Melinda, Bill had expressed his concerns about parenthood and aging. Vern Raburn, a longtime friend, recounted a 1990 conversation he's had with Bill Gates in which the latter had expressed his intrigue with how having children makes one old. Of course, he got over his reservations and fathered three children.

Chapter 15: Bill Gates Philanthropy

In the year 2000, the William H. Gates Foundation was merged with the Gates Learning Foundation, which started years prior to support educational courses, to form the Bill & Melinda Gates Foundation. This new and advanced charity organization expanded its interests from education and healthcare to include the fight against poverty as a key objective. Through the years, the foundations activities have expanded to encompass a whole range of interest like clean drinking water, toilet facilities, and clean energy, among others.

The first capital endowment to the Bill & Melinda Gates foundation consisted of about $5 billion in Microsoft stock donated by Bill Gates. Its first activities included the construction of houses for homeless people around the Puget area of Washington DC. The overarching objective of the Bill & Melinda Gates Foundation was stated as tackling global problems neglected by world governments and charitable organizations.

While the US had been polio-free for close to a century by 2000, other countries, especially in the third world, were still languishing in these and other preventable diseases. Vaccination had been a key issue for the William H. Gates foundation to tackle throughout the late 1990s. Bill would travel to countries like India and administer the vaccines himself, further increasing awareness for the fight against polio by increasing publicity for the menace.

With more of his time freed up from Microsoft to focus on his charity work, Bill displayed the same enthusiasm he had displayed for the company in the early years. He would also help position the foundation to allow maximum cooperation with the United Nations in achieving its Millennium Development Goals, which aligned with the foundation's own objectives. Bill Gates discussed his vision for a world without polio and donated to vaccination efforts all over the world.

As part of the foundation's education support efforts, libraries all over the country and around the world were connected with internet repositories for improved information access. A total of 11,000 libraries in all 50 states of America and about 50,000 computers benefited from the computerization efforts. Bill Gates believed that personal computing could be used to increase productivity and alleviate some of the world's greatest challenges by empowering people affected by those challenges to overcome them. The foundation's donations to science and education courses were also informed by this belief that education could be used as a tool to empower poverty-stricken populations and reduce most of the suffering endured by third-world countries.

In recognition of his contributions to education, science, and research, scientists named a flower fly after him, an honor bestowed upon very few celebrities.

As their charity work continued, Bill and Melinda Gates were in 2002 honored with the Jefferson Award for Greatest Public Service Benefiting the Disadvantaged for their efforts to eradicate poverty, fight disease, and promote education programs among the less privileged in North and South America as well as Africa, India, and the rest of the world.

Bill Gates had first met Warren Buffett back in 1993 during a Fourth of July party thrown by Bill's parents. The two connected over their mutual love for mathematics and their respective business interests. It would be the beginning of long and successful friendships as the two men accumulated wealth and featured consistently in lists such as Forbes' richest people in the world. Warren Buffett had built a reputation as a very sharp venture capitalist, funding numerous profitable businesses through his venture investment company, Berkshire Hathaway, from which he had accumulated a personal fortune to rival that of Chairman Bill.

In 2004, Bill Gates was invited to join the board of Berkshire Hathaway as a director. It is unclear if Bill Gates borrowed the ideas of venture capital investment from Berkshire, but the Bill & Melinda Gates foundation has definitely adopted some aspects of angel investment in its giving, ensuring that money will always be flowing into its coffers even as social enterprises fulfil whatever critical needs for which they are needed by the public.

In 2004, Bill Gates was the chairman of one of the biggest companies in America by market capitalization (about $600 billion). He was also a co-chair and trustee of the world's second richest charitable organization as well as having investments in several companies made through his venture capital firm Cascade Investment. From his personal wealth, the influence of Microsoft Corporation, and the endowment of the Bill & Melinda Gates

Foundation, Bill controlled roughly $150 billion. It is no wonder therefore, that Time magazine named Gates one of the most influential people of the year 2004 as well as the 20th century.

The next year, he would be recognized alongside his wife and U2 band leader Bono as Persons of the Year 2005 by the same Time magazine. The three have all engaged in charitable activities in response to world problems in different capacities.

Starting in 2005, Bill and Melinda had shifted their focus to sanitary solutions for the poorest populations in the world. Bill Gates talks up a new type of toilet that he expects to drastically improve the sanitary health of people who lack toilets, especially in overcrowded areas in ghettos.

With Duke University, Colorado State University, and the US Naval Research Center, Bill and Melinda Gates started the "Reinvent the Toilet Challenge" which was played out in the media for increased publicity. However, there was more to the initiative than publicity to mitigation efforts for the 2.4 billion men, women, and children around the world who do not have proper sanitation facilities.

The challenge gave rise to one of the BMGF's most ambitious projects to date; a sewage treatment plant that uses advanced biological and chemical technologies to treat raw fecal matter to produce various products, like drinking water, electricity, and a range of products that can be created from sewage sludge such as fertilizer and chemicals. The Omniprocessor has been installed in several locations in America and Africa on an introductory basis. Cheaper than conventional water treatment plants and producing much more than just safe drinking water, the Omniprocessor was hailed by Bill as the future of clean drinking water in Africa.

The Reinvent the Toilet Challenge brought together scientists to create a waste treatment system that would generate electricity and also produce clean drinkable water from waste material. But challenges arose not in the execution of the project's objectives but in the reception of the public to these ideas. The challenge and publicity efforts served to boost recognition for the new toilet design that consists of a reinvention of the toilet to be availed for people who desperately need it. But now that drinking water was being produced from human waste, anyone with a gag reflex- which is pretty much everyone- was expressing doubts as to the drinkability of the water produced by the Omniprocessor. No matter how well the mechanism has purified the water, it would be inconsumable to most people with knowledge of its source.

To lessen some of the public gag reflexes concerning the drinking of water recycled from fecal matter, Bill Gates appeared on The Tonight Show Starring Jimmy Fallon on January 2015. He had two glasses of water from which they would each pick one and drink from it. One glass contained the water recycled from 'poop' and the other contained bottled water. The challenge was to see if Jimmy could tell the difference between the recycled and the normal one. Jimmy Fallon picked what he thought was the bottled water glass (it tastes great!) and Bill Gates ostensibly drank the recycled water. In the end, Bill disclosed that the taste test had been rigged and both contained recycled water all along. Jimmy Fallon is horrified, but in the end, he had managed to convince a few million people that recycled water was no different from natural water. In fact, after undergoing so many refining and cleansing processes, the recycled water may be considered safer compared to natural water that may contain microbial organisms. And of course the video of the richest man in the world and one of the best late night show hosts sipping from a glass of the water lessened a little of the reservations people have towards water produced from fecal matter.

Few people can boast of having seen the queen, leave alone met or talked with her. The knights are the queen's specially appointed missives in various fields. Just like kings consulted with their knights while plotting war strategy, so does the queen honor outstanding men and women in various fields. In 2 March 2005, Bill Gates Bill Gates was knighted by Queen Elizabeth II for his outstanding contribution to technology, business, and humanitarian work after a recommendation by the Foreign Office. Interestingly, the Queen does not use computers. Bill would join the legion of Honorary Knight Commander of the Order of the British Empire but, unfortunately, could not be referred to as 'Sir', a noble title that is reserved for knighted British citizens.

Even during his knighting ceremony, Bill Gates was coordinating with members of the royal family to pool humanitarian efforts. Speaking after the event, Bill expressed his delight at receiving the recognition, especially considering the strategic status of the UK to both Microsoft and the BMGF.

To complete his list of impressive state commendations, Bill was awarded with the President's Medal of Freedom by President Barack Obama in 2016. The award, given to him along with his wife, was in recognition to his philanthropic efforts.

The Bill & Melinda Gates also worked to boost healthcare and education in Mexico, being one of the poorer countries in North America compared to Canada and the USA. Programs like the "Un pais de lectores" (a country of readers) were responsible for changing the lives of thousands of families and empowering millions of children to pursue education to the higher levels. For their efforts, Bill Gates and his wife Melinda were awarded the Placard of the Order of the Aztec Eagle for their philanthropy in the year 2006. This insignia would be their second national level honors by a head of state.

In anticipation for Bill Gates joining the foundation the next year, the Bill & Melinda Gates Foundation underwent reorganization in 2007. The foundation was split into four divisions namely Global Development, Global Policy & Advocacy, United States, and Global Health. Each one of these divisions signify a pillar of the foundation's objectives, making it easier to tackle challenges as they arise, and also to plan and advocate for government support for their activities as well as government intervention in areas where the foundation is incapable of reaching.

At the same time, the grants given by the foundation increasingly resemble angel investments in social enterprises. The strategy works great until the Los Angeles Times ran an op-ed criticizing Bill & Melinda Gates Foundation (BMGF) for insensitivity in their operations. For example, the foundation had supported pharma companies that discriminated against the third world in the distribution of their pharmacological products. BMGF announced that it was tightening its social responsibility evaluations to ensure that such a mistake would never happen again.

And finally, in the year 2007, Bill Gates graduated from Harvard University after a 30-year leave of absence. The honorary degree in law was awarded in June of 2007. Even though it had not been his course, Bill expressed satisfaction in having a college degree in his resume, especially with his impending job change from Microsoft employee to full-time philanthropist. In his acceptance speech, Bill encouraged the graduates to strive for social change and avoid growing complacent to the suffering of others. The best advances in humanity, Bill said, were not discoveries and scientific findings but the applications of those discoveries to bring about positive change to humanity. He also intimated that the passion he had displayed in selling software at Microsoft would now be applied to his charitable courses of improving health, alleviating poverty, and increasing access to technology for those who are unable to do so.

After the Harvard commencement speech, Warren Buffett approached Bill Gates with the biggest donation BMGF had ever received- even from Bill himself while forming it. A $30 billion stock donation paid out over a period of several years that would almost double the capital endowment of the foundation. Warren and Bill would also start coordinating in their charitable efforts based on mutual beliefs.

In 2010, Warren Buffett and Bill Gates established The Giving Pledge. While the two had already made a personal promise to give a majority of their wealth to philanthropic causes, with The Giving Pledge, they embarked on a campaign to convince other wealthy individuals to give too. Warren Buffett was already on course to achieving this objective of being one of BMGF's most generous contributors.

But The Giving Pledge was not a commitment to give to the BMGF. In fact, it was registered as a separate charitable organization. Rather than dictate to the members how to use their donations, or legally enforcing pledges, The Giving Pledge simply promotes the wisdom espoused by Carnegie about the moral obligation of rich people to share their money with the poor. By the start of the year 2019, a total of 187 people worth a combined $735 billion had signed up, pledging over $367.5 billion worth of donations. This makes the Giving Pledge one of the most lucrative charitable initiates in the history of philanthropy.

Shortly after registering The Giving Pledge in 2010, a very life-changing book was released by Houghton Mifflin Harcourt publishers. It was a book detailing the Salwen Family's story, an inspirational tale of sacrificing one's comfort to make other people's lives better. Starting in 2006, the Salwen's had discussed selling their $2 million house in Ansley Park, Georgia for one priced at half the value of their current one and give the rest of that money to charity. While the book's story arch focuses on how the process of deciding to sell the house, looking for a buyer, identifying a charitable cause to give to, and finding a new home to move to brought the family closer together, it inspired a wave of charitable giving across the country.

The Gates were inspired by the story and they invited Joan Salwen to hear more about their concepts of the "the power of half," the philosophy that had prompted her and her family to buy a house half as expensive and less than half the size of their old one. Theirs was an inspirational story to Bill Gates; after all he had not sacrificed any personal comforts to engage in charitable activities. By the end of the year, he and Warren Buffett had been joined in The Giving Pledge by Facebook CEO Mark Zuckerberg, the third richest person to sign up after Bill Gates and Warren Buffett.

Around 2010, BMGF was involved in a couple of projects to increase food reliability through improved rice yields through genetic modification research in India. Higher yield, more persistent to weather changes, and more nutritious seeds were distributed to farmers and technical support offered for the first few crop-cycles, training farmers on best farming practices. The foundation's polio vaccinations campaign was also in progress and Bill visited vaccination centers to observe. The relationship between dire poverty and susceptibility to disease and poor health is very high. A program of empowerment not only alleviates poverty; it also does so in a very dignified manner for the people concerned. In the end, the BMGF had empowered whole villages to fight poverty and lack of proper nutrition. These types of aid through empowerment by economic stimulus are very resonant with government policies.

A 2010 challenge to the global health communities for more action towards the elimination of polio in the 2010-2020 decade had also been well received. The decade was declared a Decade of Vaccines, with Polio elimination key among the objectives of this global drive. Through the actions of the Bill & Melinda Gates Foundation, including a $3 billion contribution to the effort, and the world communities, India, one of the key areas for charity efforts by the foundation, was declared polio-free in 2013 by WHO. With all these spirited contributions to alleviating human suffering at all levels, Bill Gates' influence in the world was rising. By 2012, he was fourth on the list of the world's most influential persons, one spot up from his position a year before.

The listing as one of the world's most powerful individual makes a lot of sense once you look into Bill Gates' talking points and calendar since leaving Microsoft. He has displayed a very firm and well-thought grasp of practically every global issue in numerous appearances on YouTube, televisions, and conventions. Bill Gates has become a world citizen by every definition of the word. In his role as a high profile private citizen, Bill Gates displays the outspokenness that characterized his whole business career. "If he thinks it, he will say it" seems like an accurate portrayal of his private citizen activism for issues ranging from education, healthcare, politics, energy, global warming, and foreign policy, among others.

On education, Bill discussed with Sal Khan the future of learning especially in the face of rising popularity for online education programs. In his view, the availability of thousands of learning material in video and other interactive content online has the capacity to reach more people than traditional brick-and-mortar establishments, but there is a need to keep quality high. The future of learning should incorporate virtual learning and the classroom environment aspects of peer-to-peer learning, which is the most important aspect of education.

Having discovered his passion for programming through an initiative of Lakeside School, Bill Gates appreciates the importance of co-curricular activities in building a well-rounded student. In a Money article in 2018, Bill credited his entry into programming through the Lakeside computer program to his vast wealth and success. Recognizing that not all students have the privilege of attending a private school like he did, he has made it his mission to improve the quality of education in all public schools to give every underprivileged child the opportunities that children in private schools like Lakeside get.

In an interview with CNN journalist Fareed Zakaria, Bill insisted that there was no justification for failing to support educational programs to ensure that more students can pursue education to higher levels. An advanced economy like America, Bill states, requires more specialized skills as opposed to industrial economies that require a few highly skilled individuals and many more unskilled laborers. Interventions should be focused on improving what is wrong about American education policies rather than overhauling because the United States have their own unique challenges, especially to do with size.

Another area that Bill Gates has become very involved in is the generation of clean power and reduction of environmentally harmful means like fossil fuel. Through his venture capital firm Cascade Investments, Bill invested in a nuclear energy company named TerraPower that seeks to use depleted nuclear material to produce energy. The company, still in its research phase, has come up with a bold plan to productively use the millions of tons of nuclear waste currently stockpiled in nuclear silos around the country. Its fast nuclear technology promises a payload of about 3.375 MW per metric ton of waste. To put that in perspective, it would take just 8 metric tons to power 2.5 million households for a whole year.

Bill Gates has displayed almost the same commitment to TerraPower as he showed while building Microsoft in the 80s. Unlike many of the investments in his Cascade portfolio, Bill sits at the TerraPower board as its chairman. TerraPower remains at the forefront of Bill Gates' commitment to increase energy self-reliance for developing nations.

In 2012, he discussed the world's energy deficiencies and the negative impacts of unreliable power connection on developing economies alongside Daniel Yergin, a Pulitzer-prize writer whose books focus on energy and its impact on economic activities. Bill Gates made the observation that developing world countries are being forced to use power sources that pollute and, lacking in sustainable energy sources, experience difficulties establishing industries to boost their economic well-being. Cheap renewable energy, he insists, will empower growth in the world's poorest regions and create numerous opportunities for economic empowerment. And in 2016, aside from his efforts with the Bill & Melinda Gates Foundation, Bill launched a $1 billion venture fund called the Breakthrough Energy Ventures Fund to back research and innovations in clean energy technology.

On global warming, Bill Gates decided to back a rather controversial route; chemtrails to cool the earth in addition to the reduction of greenhouse gas emission. According to Jeff Tollefson of the scientific Springer Nature, Chemtrails work by mirroring the effects of a volcanic eruption to cool the earth by releasing particles into the atmosphere to reflect the rays of the sun into space. While many people consider the idea too risky because it might change rainfall patterns among other ecological harms, proponents argue that the quick turnaround times of chemtrails make it worthwhile. Bill Gates has been bankrolled the research by Harvard atmospheric scientists James Anderson and experimental physicist

David Keith since 2009.

In similar fashion to his and Warren Buffett's efforts to bring other people on board their Giving Pledge, Bill Gates also established the Breakthrough Energy Coalition to consolidate the efforts of investors towards creating a green energy world order and, more importantly, to reduce greenhouse gas emissions. His green energy initiative has received backing from the United Nations as well as a number of countries.

Bill Gates' philanthropic efforts have not been reserved for the foundation activities. As a high profile individual, Bill has sought to use his celebrity status to encourage debate on critical issues in America and around the world. During the financial crisis in 2012, Bill Gates and Warren Buffett discussed with Charlie Rose, a Public Broadcasting Service talk show host, the impact of economic crises on the poor countries that depend on foreign aid and trade with stronger countries like America. These countries, they said, suffer the most because not only do they lack the aid that allows them to grow their economies, they also suffer from the reduced trade volumes, bringing their national output down even more.

In 2016, Bill Gates and his wife Melinda were reportedly considered as running mates for the Hillary Clinton presidential run before she settled on Senator Tim Kaine. A life in politics is not one Bill Gates would be eager to pursue as he explained on a Reddit "Ask Me Anything" (AMA) session shortly before the 2016 presidential election. An ardent admirer suggested that Bill Gates would be perfect for the job, given his vast experience running Microsoft, but Bill replied that he had no interest in a presidential run back then or in 2020.

Bill Gates prefers to spend his time solving the problems of the world without being entangled in political battles. In his view, people no longer expect much from the government. Instead local groups, he believes, are best placed to solve their own problems. Yeah, that is where Bill Gates is at now. And while speculating a 2020 presidential run may not be a big deal (anyone can suggest anyone they admire to run) the fact that he was on the shortlist for Democratic vice-presidential candidate and he is listed in practically every magazine as being one of the ten most influential persons in the world sure is.

His 64 years have been pretty incredible so far,

but I think it's safe to assume that we have not seen the highest level Bill Gates can climb to.

THE END.

Bibliography

Wallace, J. & Erickson, J. (1992). Hard drive: Bill Gates and the making of the Microsoft empire. Detroit: Wiley publishers

Gates, B. (2019). About Bill. *Gatesnotes*. https://www.gatesnotes.com/Bio retrieved on April 62019

Gates B. & Gates, M. (2019). A tradition of giving. *Bill & Melinda Gates Foundation*. https://www.gatesfoundation.org/Who-We-Are/General-Information/History retrieved April 6 2019

Bill Gates Biography: Success Story of Microsoft Co-Founder. (2019). *Astrum People website*. https://astrumpeople.com/bill-gates-biography/ retrieved April 6 2019

Wired Staff. (1998). The rise and rise of the Redmond Empire. *Wired*. https://wired.com/1998/12/redmond/amp retrieved April 6 2019

Brittlebank, W. (2016). Bill Gates launches clean energy venture fund. *Climate Action*. *http://www.climateaction.org/* retrieved on 6th April 2019

Dmitry, B. (2018). Bill Gates announces plans to use 'chemtrails' to 'solve global warming.' *News Punch.*
https://newspunch.com/author/baxter/ retrieved on 6th April 2019

Hobler, E. (2010). The Power of Half: how Hannah Salwen and her family gave half their home away. *The Telegraph.*
https://www.telegraph.co.uk/ retrieved on 6th April 2019

Belludi, N. (2015) Bill Gates and the browser wars: A case study in determination and competitive ferocity. *Right Attitude.*
http://www.rightattitudes.com/author/admin/ retrieved on 6th April 2019

Made in the USA
Coppell, TX
18 November 2020

41605929R00150